BIG DATA

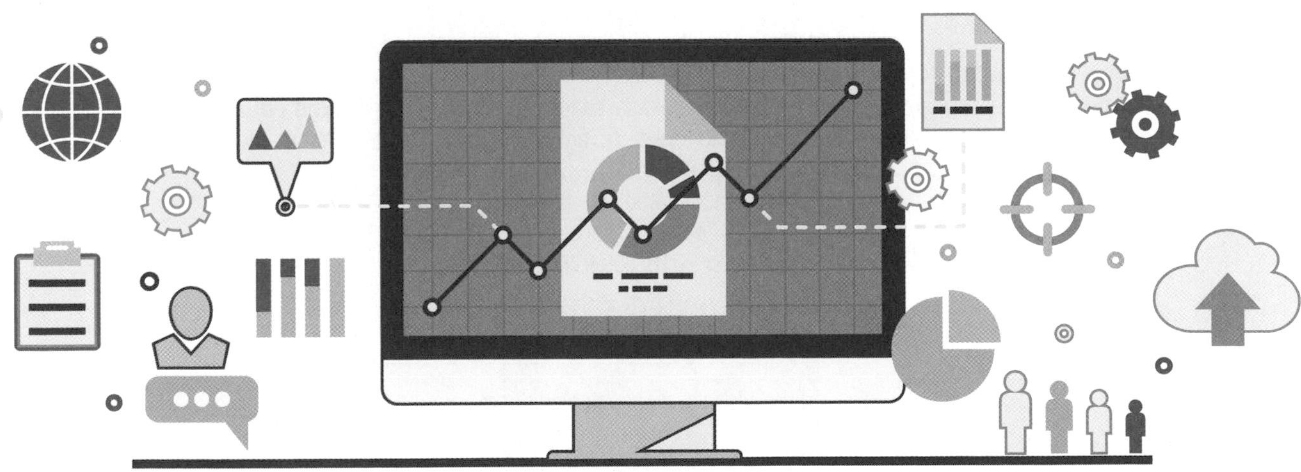

Information in the Digital World

with Science Activities for Kids

CARLA MOONEY

ILLUSTRATED BY ALEXIS CORNELL

Titles in the **Technology Today** book set

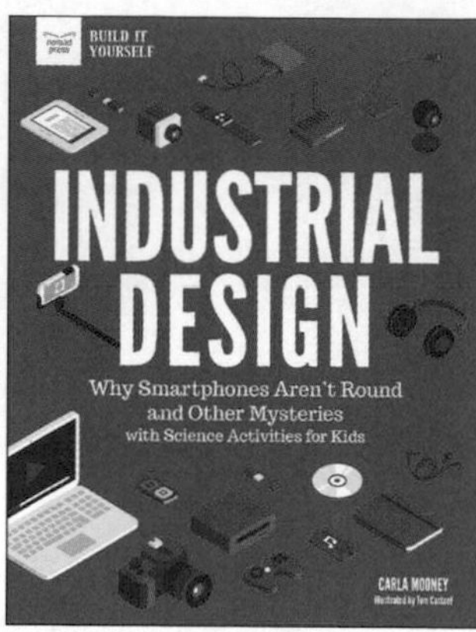

Nomad Press
A division of Nomad Communications
10 9 8 7 6 5 4 3 2 1

This book was manufactured by Friesens Book Division
Altona, MB, Canada
August 2018, Job #244120

ISBN Softcover: 978-1-61930-681-3
ISBN Hardcover: 978-1-61930-679-0

Educational Consultant, Marla Conn

Questions regarding the ordering of this book should be addressed to
Nomad Press
2456 Christian St.
White River Junction, VT 05001
www.nomadpress.net

Printed in Canada.

Contents

Timeline . . . iv

Introduction
What Is Big Data? . . . 1

Chapter 1
Where Does Data Come From? . . . 8

Chapter 2
The Transition from Paper to Computers . . . 18

Chapter 3
How Computers Store Data . . . 38

Chapter 4
Data Gets Big! . . . 59

Chapter 5
Understanding Data . . . 80

Chapter 6
The Future of Big Data . . . 100

Glossary | **Metric Conversions**
Resources | **Essential Questions** | **Index**

Interested in Primary Sources?

Look for this icon. Use a smartphone or tablet app to scan the QR code and explore more! Photos are also primary sources because a photograph takes a picture at the moment something happens.

If the QR code doesn't work, there's a list of URLs on the Resources page. Or, try searching the internet with the Keyword Prompts to find other helpful sources.

data

1085: William the Conqueror commissions a sweeping census of the British people and their property, recorded in the Domesday Book.

1820: French inventor Charles Xavier Thomas de Colmar develops the Arithmometer, one of the world's first adding machines.

1834: Charles Babbage begins the design of a new calculating machine, the Analytical Engine, which is improved on by Ada Lovelace, who is considered the first software programmer.

1874: The Remington Typewriter Co. produces the first commercially successful typewriter.

1887: Dorr E. Felt patents the Comptometer, the first commercially successful, key-driven mechanical calculator.

1890: William S. Burroughs patents his printing-adding machine.

1890: Herman Hollerith's punch card system is used to tabulate the 1890 census.

1896: Hollerith forms the Tabulating Machine Co., which would later become International Business Machines (IBM).

1936: The U.S. government orders more than 400 punch card machines from IBM to help keep track of the Social Security program.

1945: John Mauchly and J. Presper Eckert complete the Electronic Numerical Integrator and Calculator (ENIAC), an electronic computing machine. Six women program the computer.

1947: William Shockley, John Bardeen, and Walter Brattain of Bell Laboratories invent the transistor.

1952: The Universal Automatic Computer (UNIVAC) predicts Dwight D. Eisenhower as the winner of the U.S. presidential election.

1953: Grace Hopper develops the first computer language, which eventually becomes known as COBOL.

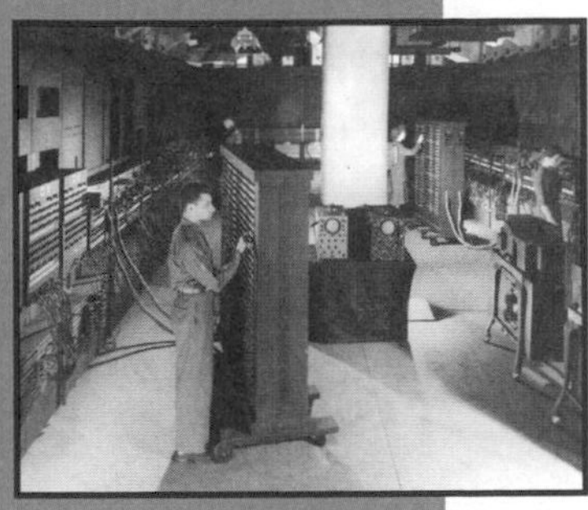

1958: Jack Kilby and Robert Noyce create an integrated circuit, known as the computer chip.

1969: The ARPAnet is the first large-scale, general-purpose computer network to connect different kinds of computers together.

1971: A team of IBM engineers invent the "floppy disk," which allows data to be shared among computers.

1981: IBM introduces its first personal computer.

1984: Phillips introduces the CD-ROM, which can hold pre-recorded data.

1991: British computer scientist Tim Berners-Lee develops the World Wide Web, a system of creating, organizing, and linking documents and Web pages on the internet.

1996: Sergey Brin and Larry Page develop the Google search engine at Stanford University.

2000: USB flash drives are introduced and used for data storage and transferring files between computers and other devices.

2003: The Blu-ray optical disc is released.

2004: Social media site Facebook is launched.

2007: Dropbox is released as a cloud-based service for convenient data storage and access to files.

2009: Google uses search query data to help the U.S. Centers for Disease Control and Prevention track the spread of the H1N1 virus.

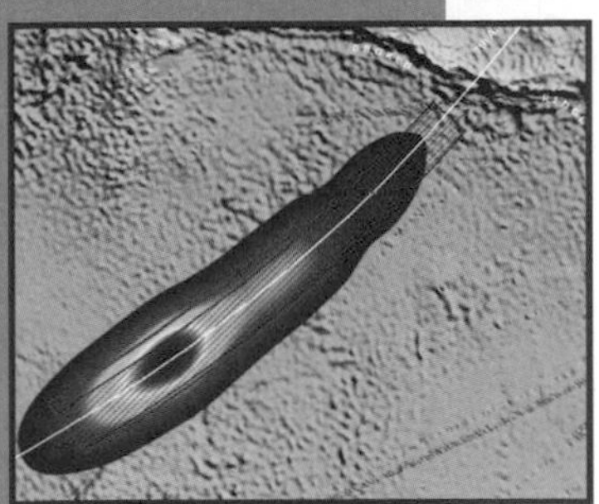

2011: Apple introduces Siri, a voice-activated personal assistant that can understand and process human language requests, as a feature with the iPhone 4S smartphone.

2017: As of the fourth quarter of 2017, Facebook has 2.2 billion monthly active users.

central processing unit
ethical
quantitative data
hacker
random access memory
database management system
structured data
decimal
outlier
platter
algorithm
concentric
keyword
artificial intelligence
pictograph
stereotype
spam filter
statistics
capacitor
fraud
tracks
morality
pixel
targeted
data point
infographic
data mining
correlation
hashtag
engineer
prototype
digital
emoji
byte
binary
data analytics
memory card
microprocessor
innovative
biomedicine
weban alytics
flash drive
big data
technology
raw data
protocols
velocity
optical storage

WHAT IS BIG DATA?

You hear the word data every day. Businesses use data to sell products, towns need data to plan for the future, and scientists create data in their experiments, for example. But what is data?

Data is a collection of small bits of information. It's what we know and can measure about the world. Data has been around since people could count and write down their observations, which means we've been creating and using data for many centuries. For example, when the ancient Romans wanted to tax the people in the Roman Empire, they used data! By counting all the people in the Roman Empire, the ancient Roman government obtained the data needed for its tax plan.

Since the introduction of the computer, data has been accumulating at an incredible pace. Today, the world holds a vast amount of **digital** data and information, and it's growing every second! There is data about how people spend their money, where people go, and what music they play. We've entered the age of **big data**.

ESSENTIAL QUESTION

In what ways does data affect your everyday life?

WHERE DOES DATA COME FROM?

What do you think of when you hear the word "data"? Many people think of a science experiment. They remember taking measurements during a lab and writing down all the observations they called data.

Scientists do create data when they perform experiments. They record both **quantitative** and **qualitative data**.

Yet scientific research is only one place that data comes from.

Data is collected every day by lots of different organizations, from businesses and governments to **nonprofit** groups and schools. Hospitals create data about illnesses, patients, and treatments. Businesses create data when they make products, provide services, and market products to customers. Governments generate data from many sources, such as **censuses**, tax filings, and **social service programs**.

DID YOU KNOW?

The Massachusetts Institute of Technology (MIT) is looking into a way to use mobile phone data about where people are and about traffic patterns to benefit **urban** planning. Using this data, the MIT researchers hope to develop best practices for stoplights, construction, and parking.

WORDS TO KNOW

data: facts and observations about something.

digital: involving the use of computer technology and presenting data as numbers.

big data: data sets that are enormous and complex.

quantitative data: facts that can be measured and reported in numbers.

qualitative data: facts about something's qualities.

nonprofit: an organization supported by donations whose main mission is to help people, animals, the environment, or other causes.

census: the process of acquiring and recording information about the members of a given population.

social service program: a program designed to promote social welfare, such as feeding and housing people living in poverty.

urban: relating to a city or large town.

innovative: introducing new ideas and creative thinking.

abundance: a very large quantity of something.

infographic: a visual representation of data, information, or knowledge.

You generate data every day in your own life. When you go shopping, you create data about what you buy. When you listen to music, you create data about the type of songs you prefer. Cell phones, computers, and fitness trackers all create data about where you go, who you text, what websites you visit, and how much you move every day. Think about it—there's not much you do that doesn't create data in some way!

THE POWER OF DATA

Many organizations have used data in **innovative** ways to help create new products and processes that improve the quality of life for people around the world. Others have used data for financial gain. Data can be used for many different purposes. At the same time, the **abundance** of data in the world today has introduced new problems.

Digital Data

According to computer software company DOMO's Data Never Sleeps 2017 survey, the amount of data being generated in the digital world is incredible. Look at where some of it is coming from every *minute*.

- **The Weather Channel:** 18,055,555,56 requests
- **Google:** 3,607,080 searches
- **Instagram:** 46,740 photos posted
- **Texting:** 15,220,700 texts sent
- **YouTube:** 4,146,600 videos watched
- **Twitter:** 456,000 tweets sent

You can view an **infographic** with more information on data at this website.

DOMO never sleeps

WORDS TO KNOW

prototype: a model of something that allows engineers to test their idea.

For example, computer scientists wonder if we have enough storage space for the vast amounts of data being created every day.

When managed and used properly, data can be a powerful tool to benefit people around the world.

As more and more of our daily lives become connected to computers, they are required to handle more and more data. Businesses used to build huge warehouses filled with computers whose only job was to store information. This was expensive and not very efficient!

DID YOU KNOW?

Retail giant Walmart handles more than 1 million customer transactions every hour, sending data to a database with each one. That's a lot of data!

Now, new improvements in data storage mean that there are fewer limits on the amount of data businesses can store. But what does that mean for users? Do people need all of this information or are we storing data we'll never use again simply because we can?

Beyond storage, other questions remain. Do we have the tools we need to capture, process, and share all of this information? And how can we keep our data secure and protect our privacy?

In *Big Data: Information in the Digital World with Science Activities for Kids*, you will explore the relationship between data, computers, and people. You'll learn about the history of data, the transition from paper to computers, and the role that search machines such as Google play in handling data. You'll see what data management means for people and how big data affects science, schools, and governments.

Get ready to start gathering data!

Engineering Design Process

Every engineer keeps a notebook to keep track of their ideas and their steps in the engineering design process. As you read through this book and do the activities, keep track of your observations, data, and designs in an engineering design worksheet, like the one shown here. When doing an activity, remember that there is no right answer or right way to approach a project. Be creative and have fun!

Problem: What problem are we trying to solve?
Research: Has anything been invented to help solve the problem? What can we learn?
Question: Are there any special requirements for the device? An example of this is a car that must go a certain distance in a certain amount of time.
Brainstorm: Draw lots of designs for your device and list the materials you are using!
Prototype: Build the design you drew during brainstorming.
Test: Test your **prototype** and record your observations.
Evaluate: Analyze your test results. Do you need to make adjustments? Do you need to try a different prototype?

Each chapter of this book begins with an essential question to help guide your exploration of big data. Keep the question in your mind as you read the chapter. At the end of each chapter, use your engineering notebook to record your thoughts and answers.

ESSENTIAL QUESTION

In what ways does data affect your everyday life?

Activity

WHERE'S THE DATA?

Data can be found everywhere in the world. You generate data about yourself everyday—at home, at school, at work, and with your friends. In this activity, you will collect data about yourself and others. Then you'll use the data you have collected to create meaningful information.

To start, find a partner—a classmate, friend, or family member—who is willing to participate in the activity with you. Together with your partner, brainstorm sources of data about each of you. Here are some ideas for data sources.

* What data can you discover about a person from their cell phone?
* What data can you discover about a person from their computer history?
* What data can you discover about a person from their schedule and activities?
* What can you discover from social media sites?

Now that you've identified several sources of data, you and your partner should select three sources from which to collect data about the other person. Decide how you are going to record or log this data—by hand, in a spreadsheet, or in a Word document. Collect and record your data.

Once you have three data sets about your subject, what can you do with the raw data? Is it meaningful in its raw format? Why or why not?

How can you organize the data so that it is more useful? What information can you learn from the data you have collected? For example, can you use the data to discover your partner's favorite hobbies, websites, or television shows? What does this tell you about your partner? Is this information accurate?

Consider This!

As more devices collect data about your activities online and offline, what issues do you think this could cause? Who sees and owns this data? What should they be allowed to do with the data? What restrictions should be put in place?

Activity

DESIGN A POLL

Often, data is collected using a poll or survey. A poll or survey asks questions about people's opinions on a topic. In this activity, you will design and conduct your own poll.

❯ **To begin, brainstorm a topic for the poll.** People conduct polls on a wide variety of topics, from sports and hobbies to politics and finances. The chosen topic should be meaningful and provide data that you can use to make a decision or answer a question.

❯ **Once you have selected a topic, think about the following questions.**

* Why did you pick this topic?
* What type of data and information do you need to answer your question?
* How will you use the data you collect?
* What question are you trying to answer?

❯ **Create a list of poll questions.** You can use multiple-choice, true-false, rating on a scale, or fill-in-the-blank formats. Then, find a group of 20 people willing to participate in the poll and give them the poll questions. Collect the results.

❯ **When every participant has completed the poll, organize and analyze the results.** What information did you learn from the poll? Did the poll raise any new questions?

Consider This!

In some cases, the results of a poll can be inaccurate. How do you think this can occur? Do you think the results of your poll were accurate? What could you do to ensure that a poll is accurate?

Chapter 1

WHERE DOES DATA COME FROM?

The world is full of data. Did you make observations about the people you saw at the mall? Did you post photographs on social media? Did you upload your English essay to Google Docs? All these actions involve data. So what exactly is data and where does it come from?

Data is simply a collection of facts and **statistics**. Often, facts are collected for later reference or analysis. Data exists everywhere. The statistics from your baseball team's last game—that's data. The math homework you turned in yesterday—that's data, too. The measurements your doctor took at your last physical exam—more data. Even the notes you took describing the weather for a week are data.

ESSENTIAL QUESTION

What areas in your life involve data?

You can think of data as being a record of your observations. It is what we know about the world.

TYPES OF DATA

WORDS TO KNOW

statistics: the practice or science of collecting and analyzing numerical data in large quantities.

There are two general types of data—quantitative data and qualitative data. Quantitative data is made up of facts that can be measured and recorded with numbers, such as your height, your weight, and the length of your hair.

Qualitative data is facts about something's features. These facts can be described but cannot be measured or reported with numbers. The color of your hair and the smoothness of your dog's fur are examples of qualitative data. You cannot measure them with numbers, but you can describe their qualities.

Let's look at these examples. Are they qualitative or quantitative? Check your answers on page 12.

1. Age of your dog
2. Number of chairs at your kitchen table
3. Color of the carpet in your family room
4. Number of dollars in your wallet
5. Smell of your shampoo

Governments collect quantitative data on every person living in the country. Why might this be helpful?

WORDS TO KNOW

technology: the scientific or mechanical tools, methods, and systems used to solve a problem or do work.

unprecedented: never done or known before.

monitor: to watch or keep track of something or someone.

search engine: a program that searches for the keywords identified by the user.

byte: a group of eight bits that is treated as a single piece of information.

analyze: to study and examine.

actuary: a person who compiles and analyzes statistics and uses them to calculate insurance risks and premiums.

insurance: a contract in which an individual or entity receives financial protection or reimbursement against losses from an insurance company.

DIGITAL DATA OVERDRIVE

In the digital age, data creation has jumped into overdrive. **Technology** is one of the biggest drivers of the increase in data. As more powerful and affordable digital devices hit the market, they are generating digital data at an **unprecedented** pace. Fitness trackers, GPS devices, laptops, tablets, smartphones, and smartwatches are just a few examples of devices that create digital data. Appliances with built-in **monitoring** systems create data about performance, usage, and repair history.

We create digital data by shopping with credit cards, using online **search engines**, social networking, and sharing online videos. Businesses and governments create data daily through many digital tools, such as online security cameras, electronic record-keeping, email, automated production and manufacturing systems, and more.

Digital data is being generated at an unbelievable pace. According to some estimates, 90 percent of data in the world today has been created in only the past two years!

Currently, about 2.5 quintillion **bytes** of data are generated each day, flowing out of the dozens of connected devices that we each use daily.

For example, when the Sloan Digital Sky Survey—a telescope survey project—started in 2000, its telescope in New Mexico collected more data in a few weeks than had been collected in the entire history of astronomy.

As the world becomes more digitally connected, more and more data will be generated in the upcoming years. From tweets and likes to swipes and shares, the digital world is expected to be teeming with data for a long time.

DID YOU KNOW?

Data can be stored in many places, including in books or magazines, on graph paper, or in computers.

USING DATA

What can we do with all this data? It's one thing to collect it, but it's a lot harder to put data to good use. For years, people have measured, collected, processed, and **analyzed** data to create information. Governments have collected census data to plan for their citizens.

Businesspeople called **actuaries** have collected data about risks to create **insurance** products. Scientists have collected and analyzed data to better understand the world around us.

A photo of the Whirlpool Galaxy, a piece of data made possible by the Sloan Digital Sky Survey

credit: Sloan Digital Sky Survey (CC BY 2.0)

WORDS TO KNOW

influence: to affect the character, development, or outcome of something.

global positioning system (GPS): a system of satellites, computers, and receivers that can determine the exact location of a receiver anywhere on the planet.

data point: a discrete unit of information.

diagnose: to determine the identity and cause of a disease or problem.

raw data: facts that have not been analyzed in any way.

processed data: facts that have been edited or cleaned in some way after collection.

outlier: a person or thing apart or detached from the main body or system.

In today's digital age, we use information created by data more than ever.

Data **influences** how we work, drive, exercise, and shop. Have you ever used a **global positioning system (GPS)** or mobile maps on your phone to get directions to a friend's house or store? The GPS provides information in the form of directions. These directions are based on data. Thousands of reports and maps are scanned and used as **data points** by GPS devices to create accurate directions.

DID YOU KNOW? Some GPS devices even use real-time data, such as traffic and accident reports, to alert a driver to a potential slowdown coming up.

When was the last time you visited the doctor? The record of your visit was probably entered into a computer to create an electronic health record.

Answers from page 9

1. Age of your dog **(Quantitative)**
2. Number of chairs at your kitchen table **(Quantitative)**
3. Color of the carpet in your family room **(Qualitative)**
4. Number of dollars in your wallet **(Quantitative)**
5. Smell of your shampoo **(Qualitative)**

With electronic records, doctors and other medical professionals can access your health history with a few clicks on a computer keyboard. Doctors use this data to **diagnose** and treat their patients.

This electronically stored data also allows doctors and hospitals to more easily compare cases across patients and more quickly identify any health trends and potentially effective treatments. In Chapter 3, you'll read about how data helped doctors slow a dangerous flu epidemic in 2009.

Raw vs. Processed Data

Not all data is the same. Some data is raw and has not been changed since it was collected. When **raw data** is edited, cleaned, or modified in any way, it becomes **processed data**. In some cases, people will process raw data to remove **outliers** or other errors that might affect results when the data is analyzed.

Data such as your blood pressure can be recorded by the doctor or nurse and stored electronically. It's important to keep medical records so informed decisions can be made about health care.

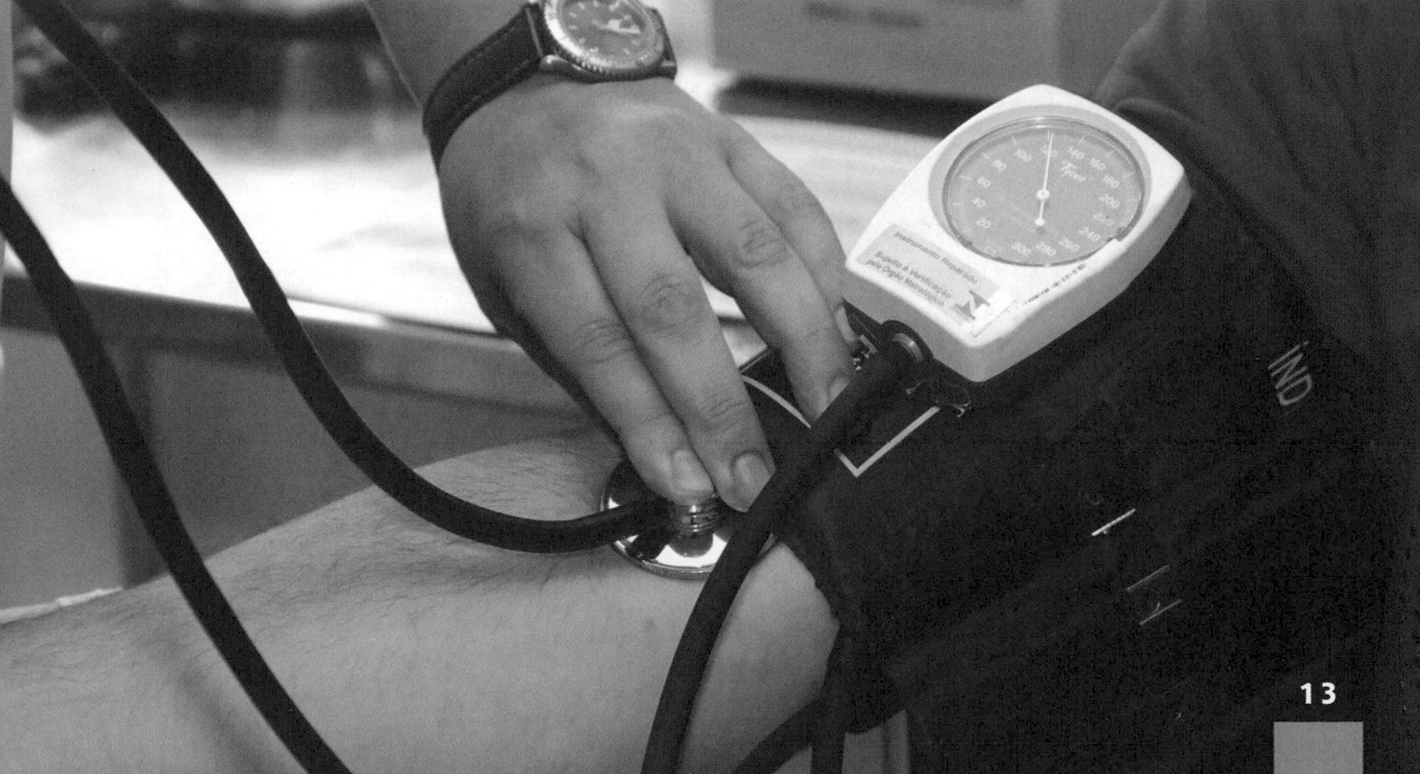

WORDS TO KNOW

wearable: an electronic device that can be worn on the body, either as an accessory or as part of material used in clothing.

Do you like to stream music? Streaming services such as Pandora and Spotify use data to deliver music that you will probably like. Every time you skip a song or indicate that you like one, a data point is created. Streaming services collect and analyze these data points across their subscribers. Streaming services use this data to create information about what style of music you will like best.

Across the country, many people wear fitness bands or watches.

These **wearables** collect data about your everyday activities. They record data such as how many steps you walk, how many flights of stairs you climb, how long you sleep, and how long you sat without moving.

The services behind these wearables analyze the data to give you information about your health. Sometimes, users can even compare their data with the data of other users and use this comparison to learn more about their health.

DID YOU KNOW?

One day, fitness wearables may send data directly to your doctors, allowing them to be involved in your health on a regular basis instead of just at an annual exam.

Many years ago, inventions such as the microscope and telescope opened new worlds that people had never been able to see before. Since then, we have added greatly to our understanding of both the microscopic world and the universe. In the same way, new inventions in data collection and analysis will give people around the world new information and help us better understand the world around us.

ESSENTIAL QUESTION

What areas in your life involve data?

Activity

QUANTITATIVE VS. QUALITATIVE DATA IN SCHOOL

Data can be quantitative or quantitative. In this activity, you'll explore how both quantitative and qualitative data can be used in decision-making.

➤ **In school, teachers can evaluate and assess students** in several different ways: letter grades, parent-teacher conferences, grade point averages, portfolios, **rubrics**, self-feedback, assessments, and more. Which ones are qualitative and which are quantitative? Make a chart to categorize each type of evaluation.

➤ **Next, think about an ideal student assessment system.** What do you think is the best way for teachers to evaluate students? Think about the following questions.

* What are the positives and negatives of using only quantitative data to assess students?
* What information might teachers miss by using only quantitative data?
* What are the positives and negatives of using only qualitative data to assess students?
* What information might teachers miss by using only qualitative data?

Try This!

Design an ideal student assessment system. Will you use quantitative data, qualitative data, or a combination of both?

WORDS TO KNOW

rubric: a guide listing specific criteria for grading or scoring academic papers, projects, or tests.

Activity

EXPLORE WEATHER DATA

What's the weather like where you live? Weather is one type of data in the world around you. It can be measured and described in many ways, including temperature, rainfall, wind speed, and humidity levels. Every measurement is a piece of data that can be used in a variety of ways.

➤ **To start, you'll need to select two cities along with your own city.** You will be collecting weather data for all three cities during a two-week period.

➤ **Every day for two weeks, use the internet and local weather sources to collect weather data.** Consider collecting the following types of data.

- ✱ Temperature, both high and low
- ✱ Wind speed
- ✱ Wind direction
- ✱ Air pressure
- ✱ Sky conditions–sunny, cloudy, partly cloudy
- ✱ Precipitation–type and amount
- ✱ Humidity

➤ **Meteorologists and other scientists use graphs and charts to look for trends in data.** Create graphs for each category of weather data to compare and contrast the data from the three cities. Need help with graphs? Try this website!

- ✱ Line graphs show gradual changes in data and are helpful for showing the relationship between different pieces of data. Create a separate line graph for each city and include temperature and wind direction data. Create another group of line graphs comparing air pressure and time for each city.

- ✱ Circle graphs show the frequency of data. Use a circle graph for each city to show sky conditions.

- ✱ Bar graphs can be used to compare data and show how something changes through time. Create a bar graph for each city using precipitation data.

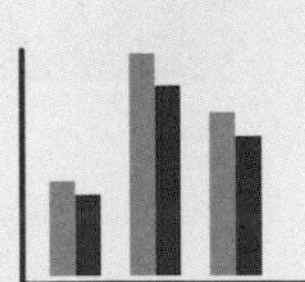

WORDS TO KNOW

humidity: the amount of moisture in the air.

Activity

Now that you have organized your weather data, you can analyze it for useful information about the weather in the three cities. Use the graphs and charts to think about the following questions.

DID YOU KNOW?

According to the Guinness Book of World Records, in 1988 scientist Nancy Knight discovered two snowflakes that looked exactly alike under a microscope. Ever since, people have been debating whether these snowflakes were identical, or if they were different enough to keep them from being an exact match.

* How would you describe the temperature changes in each city?
* What was the highest and lowest temperature in each city and when did it occur?
* What was the average temperature in each city?
* Which city had the most sunny days, cloudy days, and rainy days?
* Is there a relationship between sky conditions and temperature?
* Is there a relationship between wind direction and temperature?
* Which day had the most precipitation? Which had the least?
* What was the total precipitation for the two-week period in each city?
* How did air pressure change in each city? Did you spot any trends?
* Is there a relationship between air pressure and the sky conditions of the next day?

Data can help us better understand the world around us. How are you able to use the data you collected to better understand the weather in your city and the other cities you tracked? What can you do with this information?

Try This!

How can you use your weather data to predict future weather? Based on the graphs and data analysis that you completed in this activity, what information have you learned that could help you predict weather in your city?

Chapter 2

THE TRANSITION FROM PAPER TO COMPUTERS

We now live in a world with lots of digital data, but people have been collecting data since long before computers were invented. Some of the earliest records date back to 5000 BCE, when Sumerian merchants used clay beads to keep records of goods for sale.

More than 5,000 years ago, people living in **Mesopotamia** invented a system of writing so they could record and communicate data. Some of the earliest writing was in the form of a **pictograph**, which is a picture used to represent a word or phrase. People drew pictographs to record information about crops and taxes. As time went by, these pictographs **evolved** into a script called **cuneiform**. Mesopotamian **scribes** wrote in cuneiform on clay tablets to record data about daily events, trade, astronomy, and more. It was some of the world's first recorded data!

ESSENTIAL QUESTION

What might the world be like if we were still using pen and paper to record all our data?

EARLY PAPER RECORDS

Paper was invented in ancient China around the first century CE, and quickly became the first choice for recording data. People carefully handwrote records, descriptions, numbers, and more on pieces of paper. This method wasn't too bad if there wasn't a lot of data to be recorded. If only a few hundred people were living in a village, it wasn't hard to write down everyone's name along with a few details about their property and land.

But what if a town was home to thousands of people? That would be a lot of writing and a lot of paper!

WORDS TO KNOW

BCE: put after a date, BCE stands for Before Common Era and counts down to zero. CE stands for Common Era and counts up from zero. These nonreligious terms correspond to BC and AD. This book was printed in 2018 CE.

Sumerian: a group of people living in ancient Mesopotamia, which is modern-day Iraq.

Mesopotamia: an ancient civilization located between the Tigris and Euphrates Rivers, in what today is part of Iraq.

pictograph: the symbols in the first written languages, based on pictures instead of letters.

evolve: to change or develop gradually.

cuneiform: a system of wedge-shaped letters created by ancient civilizations.

scribe: a person who copies books, letters, and other documents by hand.

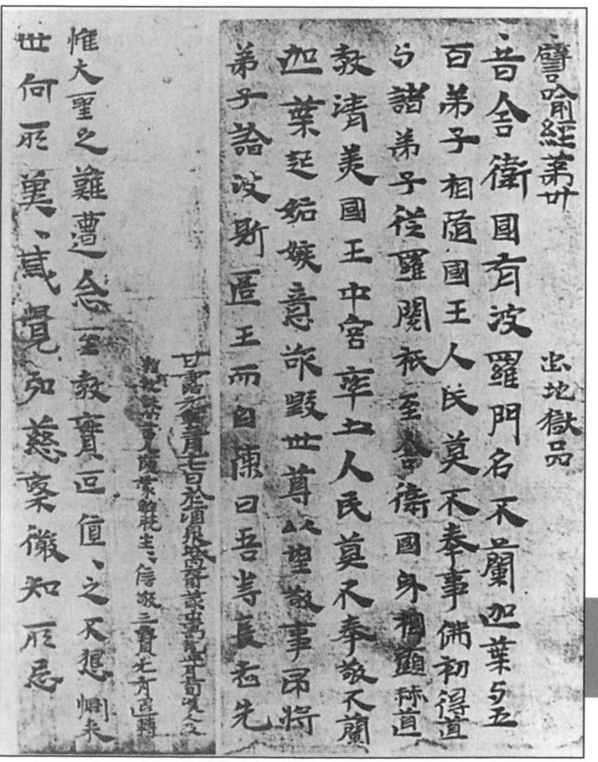

The oldest surviving paper book, the *Phi Yü Ching*, made in China around 250 BCE

Throughout history, one of the earliest data-gathering activities was a census. A census is an official count of the people in the population. Communities use a census to collect information about the citizens. In addition to counting the number of citizens, census takers also record details about the people, such as if they are male or female, married or single. The ancient Egyptians and ancient Chinese are believed to have conducted censuses.

WORDS TO KNOW

commission: an instruction given to another person, such as an artist, for a piece of work.

estimate: to form a general idea about the value, size, or cost of something.

tenant: someone who pays rent to use land or buildings owned by someone else.

decimal: a number system based on units of 10.

punch card: a card with holes punched in it that gives directions to a machine or computer.

tabulate: to count, record, or list data in a systematic way.

tally: to count the number of something.

In 1085, the king of England, William the Conqueror, **commissioned** a survey of the English people, their land, and property. He wanted to have data about the land and property owned by the English people so he could **estimate** the amount of taxes he could collect from them.

For almost a year, royal representatives spread across the country gathering data about the people. They recorded this data by hand in more than 900 pages in two large books—the Great Domesday and the Little Domesday—known together as the Domesday Book.

DID YOU KNOW?

One of the earliest counting methods was the human hand and fingers, able to count up to 10 objects.

The Domesday Book has extensive records of land owners, **tenants**, livestock, buildings, and other items in 13,000 places in England and parts of Wales. Europe had never conducted a survey on this scale.

William the Conqueror died in 1087, before his Domesday Book census was complete. **You can see a page and a translation from the Domesday Book online at the National Archives at this website.**

PS

National Archives Domesday

Taking a census was time-consuming and expensive. Even after spending months collecting data on the people and their property, the census takers could not count everyone and everything exactly. The data was an estimate. Still, it was better than having no data at all!

Counting Data by Abacus

The abacus was one of the earliest tools created to help people count data. An abacus consists of a frame that holds rods or wires with sliding beads mounted on them. The rods represent **decimal** places in a number. To count data, a person moved the beads on the abacus. The abacus could also be used for simple math calculations, such as addition, subtraction, multiplication, and division.

USING PUNCH CARDS

By the late nineteenth century, the population of the United States had grown so much that the U.S. Census Bureau could not keep up with the increasing amount of data. Manually counting the paper records from the 1880 census took eight years to finish! By the time the data was ready, it was already out-of-date. Even worse, the Census Bureau estimated that the 1890 census would take 13 years to complete. It would take so long to gather and count the data that it would be useless.

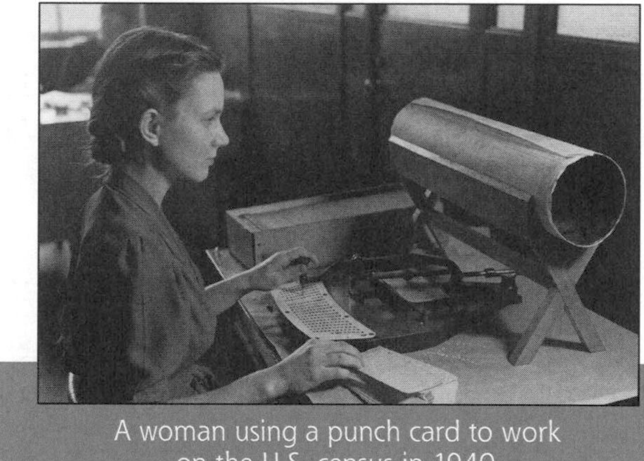

A woman using a punch card to work on the U.S. census in 1940

To find a solution, the U.S. Census Bureau reached out to Herman Hollerith (1860–1929), an American inventor. Hollerith designed a machine that used **punch cards** to automatically **tabulate** the census data. The electric tabulating machine used the location of the holes on each card to record and **tally** the data.

WORDS TO KNOW

Industrial Revolution: a period of time beginning in the late 1700s when people started using machines to make things in large factories.

carbon copy: an exact copy of a document made using carbon paper between two or more pieces of paper.

Used in the 1890 census, Hollerith's tabulation machines were a great success. They reduced the amount of time it took to process the 1890 census. However, even though it was faster than the previous census, it was still a long process.

Every person in the United States had to fill out a paper form. Then, census workers transferred the data from the forms to millions of cards by individually punching holes in the cards. Next, they stacked the cards by hand. Finally, the cards were read by tabulation machines, which counted and recorded the census data.

DID YOU KNOW?

One of the first users of the Remington typewriter was Samuel Langhorne Clemens (1835–1910), better known as the author Mark Twain. Have you read any of his books?

AMERICAN OFFICE MACHINERY

The **Industrial Revolution** drew more people to live and work in cities with the promise of factory jobs. Businesses grew and governments expanded. With all this growth, the amount of data available also increased, from census data and tax records to sales figures and customer lists. People needed new ways to collect and process large amounts of data in a reasonable amount of time.

In the United States, several types of office machinery emerged to handle data and information faster and more efficiently. Typewriters, adding machines, and punch card accounting machines appeared in offices across the country.

A typewriter from the early twentieth century

With the typewriter, documents could be created quickly and easily.

Now, offices needed a new way to store all those paper records. Before the typewriter, office workers stored handwritten documents in a letter book. An office clerk made a permanent copy of any letter being sent or received by handwriting a copy into the letter book. With the introduction of the typewriter and **carbon copies**, this process was no longer needed. Instead, the copies could be stored in filing cabinets.

The job of processing data fell to another type of office machinery—the adding machine. One of the first adding machines, called the Arithmometer, was developed in 1820 by French inventor Charles Xavier Thomas de Colmar (1785–1870).

Gutenberg's Information Revolution

Prior to the mid-fifteenth century, data and information recorded in books were printed using a woodblock printing method or carefully copied by hand. Both methods were very time-consuming. As a result, books in Europe were so expensive that most people could not afford to buy them. In the mid-fifteenth century, a German craftsman named Johannes Gutenberg (circa 1400–1468) experimented with different ways to speed up the printing process. By 1439, he developed a printing press that used moveable type. Gutenberg's press also automated the transfer of ink from movable type to paper. This first printing press made printing papers and books much more efficient than using woodblocks or handwriting. For the first time, books could be mass-produced, and information became more available to many people. Why did this make such a big difference to the world's population?

A woodcut by Swiss artist Jost Amman (1539–1591) showing an early version of the printing press

WORDS TO KNOW

Difference Engine: an early calculating machine, designed and partially built during the early 1800s by English mathematician Charles Babbage.

Analytical Engine: a proposed mechanical general-purpose computer designed by English mathematician Charles Babbage.

simultaneously: at the same time.

algorithm: a set of steps or a procedure to be followed in calculations or other problem-solving operations, especially by a computer.

programmer: a person who writes computer programs. Also called a coder.

By the late 1800s, offices needed a faster adding machine. At the same time, banks needed a permanent written record of the numbers entered. To solve these problems, two inventors—Dorr E. Felt (1862–1930) and William S. Burroughs (1855–1898)—created new adding machines, one that used keys like a typewriter and one that printed out data as it was entered in the machine.

BABBAGE'S ENGINES

Now that we know a little about the office machines that made recording and processing data a little easier, when did the computer come into the picture? There is no single inventor of the computer. Instead, many people were involved in creating the machine that we know today as a computer.

Back in the nineteenth century, an English mathematics professor named Charles Babbage (1791–1871) designed a machine that could perform calculations. Mathematical tables were needed for science, engineering, and navigation. Powered by cranking a handle, Babbage's **Difference Engine** calculated and printed mathematical tables.

A model of Babbage's Difference Engine, built in 2002, 153 years after it was designed

credit: Jitze Couperus (CC BY 2.0)

Later, Babbage designed what he called his **Analytical Engine** to be programmed with punch cards. However, Babbage's Analytical Engine was never fully completed, as the British government stopped funding his projects.

THE ELECTRONIC COMPUTER

The Atanasoff-Berry Computer (ABC) is one of the earliest examples of an electronic computer. At Iowa State University, between 1939 and 1942, professor John Vincent Atanasoff (1903–1995) and graduate student Clifford Berry (1918–1963) worked to build an electronic computing machine. Atanasoff and Berry developed a computer that could perform complex math and complete 30 operations **simultaneously**.

Ada Lovelace

Born in 1815, Augusta Ada Byron was the daughter of famed poet Lord Byron. Her mother, Lady Byron, had studied mathematics and insisted that Ada also be tutored in the subject, an unusual education for a woman in nineteenth-century England. When she was 17, Ada met inventor and mathematician Charles Babbage at a party. She observed him demonstrate a portion of his Difference Engine, a mathematical calculating machine, and she became fascinated by Babbage's engines. Years later, Ada, who became the Countess of Lovelace after marriage, published a translation of a French article on Babbage's Analytical Engine, adding extensive notes of her own to the translation.

Ada's notes included the description of a sequence of operations for solving certain mathematical problems, which some believe to be the first **algorithm** to be performed by a machine. For this reason, she is known as the world's first computer **programmer**. Ada also imagined that computers could be used for more than just performing mathematical calculations. She envisioned a machine that could manipulate all types of content, from music to pictures, in digital form. In 1979, the U.S. Department of Defense named a new computer programming language "Ada" after Lovelace.

WORDS TO KNOW

trajectory: the curve or line taken by an object moving through space.

vacuum tube: an electronic component that looks like a lightbulb and was used as an on/off switch in early computers and other appliances.

capacitor: a device that stores electrical energy until it's needed.

relay: an electrical device that is activated by a current or signal in one circuit to open or close another circuit.

engineer: a person who uses math, science, and creativity to solve problems or meet human needs.

But before the computer could be finished, the United States entered World War II and work on the ABC stopped. Even so, the development of the ABC helped pave the way for future electronic computing.

ENIAC

From 1939 to 1945, World War II raged on battlefields across Europe and the Pacific. The war triggered the development of new technologies, mostly for military use.

The U.S. military wanted to be able to speed up computations that were needed to calculate the speed and **trajectory** of bombs and missiles. Two University of Pennsylvania professors, John Mauchly (1907–1980) and J. Presper Eckert (1919–1995), began work on a high-speed electronic computing machine that could perform these calculations. They named it the Electronic Numerical Integrator and Calculator (ENIAC). When it was finished in 1946, ENIAC filled a 1,500-square-foot room, the size of an average home's first floor! The massive machine contained 18,000 **vacuum tubes**, 10,000 **capacitors**, 6,000 switches, and 1,500 **relays**.

By the time ENIAC was completed, the war was over, but ENIAC still served as the U.S. Army's primary computing machine for the next decade. Calculations that had previously taken 12 hours on a calculator could be accomplished in just 30 seconds.

DID YOU KNOW?

The primary programmers of ENIAC were Kay McNulty, Betty Jennings, Betty Snyder, Marlyn Wescoff, Fran Bilas, and Ruth Lichterman. The groundbreaking work of these six women was not recognized for more than 50 years.

In the late 1940s, a consultant on the ENIAC team, John von Neumann (1903–1957), developed a new computer. The Electronic Discrete Variable Automatic Computer (EDVAC) used a stored program concept that allowed programs to be read into the computer. It marked the beginning of general purpose computers.

ENIAC and EDVAC proved that it was possible to build a computer. Their success inspired other scientists and **engineers** to build better computers.

FIVE GENERATIONS OF COMPUTER HISTORY

The laptop you have in your backpack is very different from the early, room-sized computers such as ENIAC and EDVAC. Computers have changed and improved dramatically. Most experts divide the history of computers into five generations. Each generation is marked by an invention or development that significantly changed how the computer worked.

UNIVAC

On November 5, 1952, Americans watched television to hear the results of the presidential election between Gen. Dwight D. Eisenhower (1890–1969) and Adlai Stevenson (1900–1965). CBS news anchor Walter Cronkite (1916–2009) had a mockup of a new technology called a UNIVAC (UNIVersal Automatic Computer) next to his desk, along with its inventor J. Presper Eckert. They explained they would use the machine to predict the election's result. Earlier, U.S. Navy mathematician Grace Hopper (1906–1992) and her team had entered voting statistics from prior elections into UNIVAC and written the computer code that would predict the election's result. While many national polls predicted Stevenson would win, with only 5 percent of the vote counted, the UNIVAC predicted a victory for Eisenhower. And it was right! Eisenhower won the election.

WORDS TO KNOW

circuit: a path for electric current to flow, beginning and ending at the same point.

transistor: a small device that acts as an on/off switch to control the flow of electricity in a computer.

symbolic assembly language: a programming language that lets users relay information to computers with words instead of numbers.

binary: a math system that uses only the numbers 0 and 1.

integrated circuit: a tiny complex of electronic components and their connections on a small piece of material such as silicon.

semiconducting: a material that can only weakly conduct electricity.

parallel processing: using more than one processor in the same computer.

The first generation of computers (early 1940s–late 1950s) used vacuum tubes as **circuits** and magnetic drums for memory. These components made first-generation computers enormous. A single computer filled an entire room. Because they also used a lot of electricity and broke down frequently, these computers were expensive to run.

First-generation computers used machine language, a basic programming language, and could solve only one problem at a time. Data was input on punched cards and paper tape. The computer printed its output on paper. The ENIAC and UNIVAC computers are examples of first-generation computers.

In the late 1940s, researchers at Bell Labs developed the **transistor**. A transistor is a device that regulates the flow of electronic signals and electrical power.

In the second generation of computers (late 1950s–mid 1960s), transistors replaced vacuum tubes to conduct electrical current in the machines. They were a big improvement over vacuum tubes because they allowed computers to become smaller, faster, and cheaper, and use less electricity.

The ENIAC computer took up an entire room!

credit: U.S. Army

During this period, programming languages also improved. **Symbolic assembly languages** allowed programmers to create instructions in words instead of **binary** 0s and 1s.

In the late 1950s, the first **integrated circuit** was developed. An integrated circuit is a tiny collection of electronic components, such as resistors, transistors, and capacitors, all connected on a tiny chip made of a **semiconducting** material, such as silicon. It performs all the same functions as a larger electronic circuit made of separate components.

Integrated circuits ushered in the third generation of computers (mid 1960s–early 1970s). Integrated circuits allowed engineers to develop computers that were more powerful than previous models. At the same time, computers continued to become smaller and cheaper. Additionally, these computers had keyboards and monitors, which communicated with the computer's operating system. This was a significant change from the punch cards and printouts of the past.

The computers could run several applications at the same time, while a central operating program monitored the computer's memory.

In the early 1970s, American technology company Intel developed the Intel 4004 chip. This tiny chip ushered in the fourth generation of computers.

DID YOU KNOW?

Second-generation computers with transistors were the first machines to store instructions into their memories, using magnetic core technology.

Parallel Processing

Until recent years, most computer were serial computers. They had one processor chip that held one processor. The computer could perform only one step in a program at a time. By 2008, most new computers had more than one processor on a single chip. This allowed the computer to perform **parallel processing**, where multiple processors divide a program's instructions. This allows the computer to run a program faster.

WORDS TO KNOW

central processing unit (CPU): the part of a computer in which operations are controlled and executed.

microprocessor: a small electronic chip that manages information and controls what a computer does.

artificial intelligence (AI): the intelligence of a computer, program, or machine.

protocols: a set of rules governing the exchange or transmission of data between devices.

The Intel 4004 chip allowed computer makers to place all a computer's components—from its **central processing unit (CPU)** to its memory and input/output controls—on a single chip. This technology drastically shrank the size of computers. For the first time, **microprocessors** made it possible for companies to make computers that were small enough and affordable for home use.

The fifth generation of computers is still being developed. These computers use some incredible technologies, such as voice recognition and **artificial intelligence (AI)**. You can ask a machine a question and get an immediate answer. Engineers are working to develop machines that can process and respond to human language, as well as learn by themselves. As technology continues to improve, computers will continue to develop and change.

DID YOU KNOW?

In 1981, IBM designed the first home computer, which was quickly followed by the Apple Macintosh in 1984.

Quantum Computers

In the future, quantum computers may be used to process data. Today's computers code data using binary numbers, using a value of 0 or 1. Each individual binary number is a bit. The sequence of bits gives the computer instructions. Instead of using bits to store information, quantum computers use qubits. Quantum computers work based on two important principles of quantum physics called superposition and entanglement. Superposition means that each qubit can represent both a 0 and a 1 at the same time. Entanglement means that qubits are connected to each other. Whether one qubit is a 0 or a 1 can depend on what another qubit is. Quantum computing is still very new. Companies such as IBM and Google are working on developing quantum computers, hoping that they will be much faster and able to handle more complex data than computers today.

BIRTH OF THE INTERNET

Like computers, the internet does not have a single inventor. Instead, it evolved through the efforts of many people. In 1958, U.S. President Dwight D. Eisenhower created the Advanced Research Projects Agency (ARPA). One of ARPA's goals was to improve the country's computer science capabilities.

In the late 1950s and early 1960s, computers were used as enormous calculators, not as communication tools. Additionally, each computer operated on its own, and there were no computer networks. If two computers were running on different operating systems, they could not communicate with each other. With the help of computing experts and university scientists, ARPA devised a way for computers running on different operating systems to "talk" to each other over a network. They called the network ARPAnet. The designers developed a common set of rules, or **protocols**, that the network followed so the computers could communicate with each other. These early ARPAnet protocols evolved into many of the protocols that are used on the modern internet.

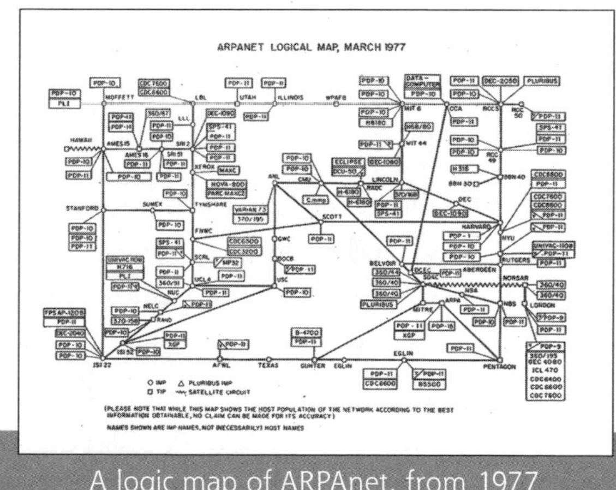

A logic map of ARPAnet, from 1977

In the 1970s and early 1980s, scientists and researchers added more computers and networks to ARPAnet. This system of communication between computers and networks became the internet.

As the internet grew, it connected millions of computers worldwide. The early internet allowed people to communicate in small groups through networks that were closed to anyone who did not have permission to use them. As decades passed, the internet became an open network, and the number of people using it also increased.

In 1991, a British computer scientist named Timothy John Berners-Lee (1955–) developed the World Wide Web, a system of creating, organizing, and linking documents and web pages. Berners-Lee also designed a web page coding system, called HTML, and an addressing system that gave each web page a specific and unique location, or URL.

The web made using the internet easier, giving users the ability to find their way around the massive network of computers. Today, we take it for granted that we can check our email or stream a movie in many ways—from a tablet, smartphone, or laptop. This wasn't always the case!

DID YOU KNOW?

HTML stands for Hyper Text Markup Language. The computer language is used to create documents on the World Wide Web incorporating text, graphics, sound, video, and hyperlinks

In addition, the development of browsers and search engines such as Internet Explorer, Safari, and Google helped people find information on the internet. Now, the internet is an important part of daily life and a massive new source of data.

Now that we know computers handle most of our data, in the next chapter we'll look at the hardware and software that make this possible.

ESSENTIAL QUESTION

What might the world be like if we were still using pen and paper to record all our data?

Activity

CHANGING HOW WE LIVE

Computers have changed how we live. They have also changed how data is generated, recorded, processed, and stored. Yet computers did not do all of this from the very beginning. Instead, many people developed new technologies and ideas that improved computers and made them the powerful machines they are today.

➤ **Find someone who remembers the 1980s and interview them about what computers were like then.** You could ask some of the following questions.

* Did they have a computer at home, at school, at work?
* How did they use computers?
* Where and when did they first use a computer?
* What was it like and what did they use it for?
* How did they do things such as writing, researching, shopping, and communicating before computers?
* How have computers made their lives easier? How have they made them harder?

➤ **Using what you learned, create a presentation to compare and contrast the computers from the 1980s with those of today.** Show how computers have changed the way we live and how we handle data.

Consider This!

Think about how computers may continue to change in the future. What new needs will they fill? How will they change from today? How will they be different and how will they be similar? What will they look like? Draw a sketch of your idea of a future computer.

Activity

TELL A STORY IN PICTOGRAPHS

One of the world's earliest forms of writing, pictographs are drawings that represent a word or phrase. Many cultures drew pictographs on cave walls, cliffs, and other surfaces to record data and information. Several pictographs could be put together to tell a story or recall an event. In this activity, you'll create your own set of pictographs to tell a story.

› **To begin, find examples of pictographs in your daily life.** Hint: How do you know which bathroom to use at a restaurant or that there is an upcoming turn in the road? Do you use any pictographs when you send a text or post on social media? Make a list of all the pictographs you discover. What does each mean?

› **Now, imagine that you need to pass data or information to other people.** Maybe you need to record instructions on how to make a sandwich or grow sunflowers in the garden. Brainstorm different ideas about the information you want to express.

› **Next, create a set of pictographs that you will use to tell your story.** Then, create a presentation—using poster board, PowerPoint, or another medium—that uses your pictographs to pass along the information.

› **Share the presentation with others.** Have them record what they believe your presentation is about. What do they think each pictograph represents? Compare your original story to their interpretation. Were there any differences? Were some pictographs interpreted in different ways by different people? Why do you think this occurred? How do you think this could affect data and information passed from generation to generation or one culture to another?

Consider This!

What pictographs are used in foreign countries? Can you understand them? In what situations might using pictographs be more effective than words?

Activity

LEARNING ABOUT COMPUTER HISTORY

Many people, discoveries, and milestones were part of the history of the computer. From counting on an abacus to designing the first computer game, many people had a role in creating the technology behind today's computers. In this activity, you'll have the chance to learn a little more about a person or discovery you find especially interesting.

❯ **To start, think about an area of computer and data history that you want to learn more about.** You can pick a topic from this list, browse through the Computer History Museum's website for ideas, or choose one of your own.

* Abacus
* Charles Babbage and Ada Lovelace
* Hollerith's punched cards
* Grace Hopper
* Colossus computer
* The six ENIAC programmers
* First IBM personal computer
* Apple Macintosh
* Microsoft Windows
* Google search engine

❯ **Using the internet and your library, research your chosen topic.** Why is your topic important? What problem did it solve? How did it contribute to computer history?

❯ **Create a short video or PowerPoint presentation to share what you learned.**

Consider This!

What is the connection between the topic you chose and how we collect, store, and use data today? How did this discovery or person in computer history impact the world of data today?

Activity

USING PUNCH CARDS TO STORE DATA

A punch card was made from a piece of stiff paper. A series of holes were punched by hand or machine in set patterns in the paper. These patterns of holes represented data. Generally, a punch card used one column of holes to represent a digit or letter. Each card could hold only a small amount of data. If you wrote a computer program using punch cards, each card contained only one line of code. The punch cards had to be kept in order in a stack. Usually, the upper corner of the cards was cut so that the cards could be easily stacked correctly.

You can see an illustration of a punch card from Hollerith's tabulating machine here, as well as an example of a punch card from Japan.

Punch cards allowed people to store and access information by entering the data on the cards into a computer. The cards were inserted into a punch card reader, which input the data from the cards into the computer. The punch card reader started at the top left of a card and read each column vertically, beginning at the top and moving down the column. Once it finished reading a column, it moved to the next column and started over. In this activity, you'll learn how punch cards work by creating your own punch card coding system.

- **Develop a system of punching that represents letters.** Write down your punching system.
- **Choose a sentence that you want to communicate.**
- **Using your punching system,** translate your sentence by making holes on index cards with a hole puncher or marker.

Activity

❯ **Make sure that you keep your punch cards in order and in the right position.**

❯ **Test to see how well your card system works.** Give your written punch code and your index cards to other people to read. Can they read your cards and understand the data? If not, what could you do to improve your punch cards?

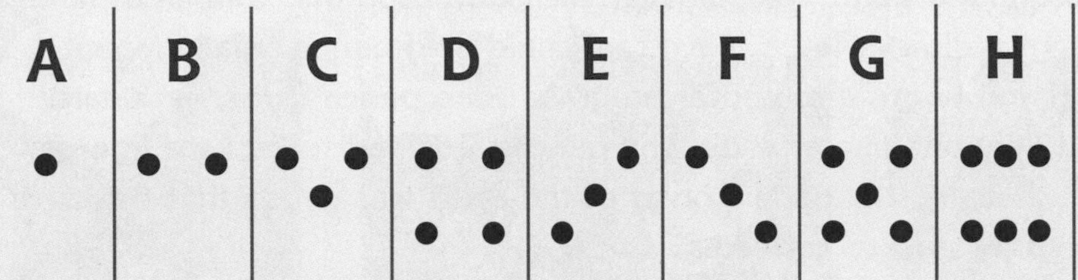

Try This!

Punch cards also need to communicate numbers and punctuation. Can you devise a system to relay different types of data on the same card?

Punch Cards are Looming

One of the first uses of punch cards happened in an industry very different from data management. In 1801, the French weaver Joseph Marie Jacquard (1752–1834) devised a system of punch cards that could be read mechanically to inform a loom what pattern should be woven into a cloth. To demonstrate how well they worked, Jacquard used 10,000 of these punch cards to "program" a loom to weave a tapestry showing his portrait in black and white silk.

Chapter 3

HOW COMPUTERS STORE DATA

When you store old papers from school, you might just shove them into a desk drawer or crumple them at the bottom of your locker. Storing data in a computer is very different.

Computers have made it a lot easier to collect, process, and store enormous amounts of data. What good is all that data if we can't get it when we need it? Every day, more people and businesses are getting rid of file cabinets stuffed with paper and are storing data electronically. So, how do computers store data?

There are many levels of storage, ranked by speed and cost. Memory and disk storage are the two largest categories. Memory is storage for data that the computer is currently working on, such as editing a document or spreadsheet or browsing the internet. Disk storage is for data that is inactive but saved for future use. When you save a document after you edit it, you can work on it again later because it is in long-term storage.

ESSENTIAL QUESTION

What would it be like to try to use data without a data management system to help you?

BINARY NUMBERS

WORDS TO KNOW

pixel: short for "picture element," one of the small squares of color used to show an image on a digital screen.

To understand storage on a computer, you need to understand binary numbers. In a computer, every piece of data is stored as numbers. If you write a research paper and save it on your computer, each letter is converted into a number. Even a photograph is converted into a large set of numbers. Each number tells the computer the color and brightness of each **pixel** in the photograph.

Every day, we use a decimal number system, also known as a base-10 system. A base-10 system uses 10 numerals—0,1,2,3,4,5,6,7,8,9—to represent numbers. If you need to write a number larger than 9, you use a combination of these numerals and place values. A place value gives each column or place in a number a certain value. In a base-10 system, each place to the left in a number increases by a power of 10. For example, let's look at the place values in this number: 2,487,395.

2,487,395

millions, hundred thousands, ten thousands, thousands, hundreds, tens, ones

Using only 10 numerals, you can create any value!

A computer, however, uses a different type of number system—a binary number system. A binary number system is a base-two system. It uses only two numerals—0 and 1—to represent all values.

The first programmable computer using binary numbers was the Z1 created by German inventor Konrad Zuse (1910–1995) between 1936 and 1938. **You can see a reconstruction of the Z1 at the German Museum of Technology at this website.**

Z1 German Museum Technology

WORDS TO KNOW

flash drive: a small, portable device that stores data.

flash technology: data storage technology that uses electrical energy to store data.

Like the base-10 system, a binary number system also uses place values. However, the place values are different. In a binary system, each place to the left increases by a factor of 2 (instead of 10). For example, look at this binary number.

1	0	0	1
8 place	4 place	2 place	1 place

This binary number has a 1 in the ones place and a 1 in the eights place. Therefore, it is the binary number for 9.

The following chart shows the decimal numbers 0 through 9 written as binary numbers. While binary numbers can be very long, they can be used to store any value.

DID YOU KNOW? In a binary number system, every individual 0 and 1 is called a "bit."

Decimal	Binary
0	0
1	1
2	10
3	11
4	100
5	101
6	110
7	111
8	1000
9	1001

History of Binary Numbers

The binary number system existed long before computers. In Australia, Aboriginal people used a base-two number system for counting. African tribes also used a binary system of high and low drum beats to send messages across far distances. And in the seventeenth century, mathematician Gottfried Wilhelm Leibniz (1664–1716) used a binary number system and showed how it could be applied in an early calculating machine.

PERMANENT STORAGE

Once the computer converts data into a string of binary numbers, what's next? To store that data, a computer uses a data storage device. In many computers, the main data storage device is a hard disk drive. The hard drive allows the computer to permanently store data in an organized way that makes it easy to retrieve when you need it. It's the hard drive in your computer that allows you to store photos, music files, and text documents.

Other times, you might use a data storage device called a **flash drive** to permanently store data. A flash drive is a small, portable device that allows you to store data and easily transfer it from computer to computer.

A data storage device such as a hard drive or flash drive is a like a dresser in your bedroom.

Each drawer holds a certain amount of clothing that you can wear in the future. When you need a shirt, you simply open the correct drawer and take one out. A computer's data storage device works in a similar way, putting data in specific places so it is easy to find and use. These drives work using different technologies, including magnetic, optical, and **flash technology**.

Computer hard drive

credit: William Warby (CC BY 2.0)

A USB flash drive

WORDS TO KNOW

magnetism: the force that attracts or repels between magnets.

platter: a large, circular plate in a magnetic hard drive that stores data via magnetic charges.

concentric: having a common center.

tracks: circular paths on the platter of a magnetic hard drive.

segment: part of something.

sectors: smaller segments of tracks on a magnetic hard drive.

read-write head: a small part of the disk drive that transforms a magnetic field into electrical current or vice versa.

MAGNETIC HARD DRIVES

Some hard drives use **magnetism** to store data. Imagine that you want to use magnetism to send a message to a friend. Each day, you leave a metal nail next to their door. Your friend knows that if the nail is magnetized, you'll be over after dinner to play video games. If the nail is not magnetized, you've got something else to do and can't come. In this way, you are using magnetism to store information and send a message.

Computers use this same idea, only in a much bigger way.

The hard disk drive is a spinning disk or disks with magnetic coatings and heads that can read and write magnetic information. The magnetic material on the hard drive is a large, circular **platter** that can be divided into billions of tiny areas.

Each area can be magnetized to store a binary 1 or demagnetized to store a binary 0. The hard drive typically remains inside a computer, laptop, or other device. It stores data permanently, so it can be retrieved later.

Flash Memory

Flash memory is a type of data storage. A secure digital (SD) card in your camera or smartphone is one example of flash memory. External solid state drives (SSD) and universal serial bus (USB) flash drives are other examples of flash memory devices. Both connect to a computer's USB port to be read from and written to.

DID YOU KNOW?

A hard drive's platter is made from a material such as glass or aluminum and coated with a thin layer of a metal that can be magnetized or demagnetized.

How does a computer read the data stored on a hard drive? Data stored on a hard drive isn't like a stack of papers on your desk. On each platter, the computer stores data in a very orderly pattern. Bits of data are arranged in **concentric**, circular paths on the platter, called **tracks**. Each track can be broken into smaller **segments** called **sectors**.

The hard drive also stores a map of sectors that are being used and the ones that are free for new data. When the computer needs to store new data, it uses the map to identify free sectors. Then it tells the hard drive's **read-write head** to move across the platter to the exact location of the sector and store the data in that place.

To retrieve data, the computer follows a similar process. It identifies the location of the data and sends the drive's read-write head to retrieve it.

The read-write head in a hard drive

WORDS TO KNOW

durable: able to last.

optical storage: a type of data storage that uses lasers to record and retrieve data.

FLASH STORAGE

Some laptop computers use flash technology to store data. Instead of using magnetism, this technology uses electrical energy to store data. Flash storage devices include SSDs and flash memory sticks. The computer records data on a memory chip by charging or not charging a series of tiny capacitors in the chip. A capacitor is a device that stores electrical energy.

Although flash storage can be more durable than magnetic storage, the capacitors can lose their ability to store electrical charges after several years.

Why do some laptops use flash memory and SSDs? This type of electronic storage has several advantages over magnetic hard drives. While a traditional magnetic hard drive has moving parts—motors that spin magnetic platters and drive heads—the storage on an SSD occurs in flash memory chips. Because no power is needed to run motors, an SSD uses much less power than a regular hard drive, which is a distinct advantage for a portable computer such as a laptop. Portable computers rely on batteries, and if the batteries run out super fast, that's a problem!

An SSD from the inside

An SSD from the outside

SSDs can access data faster because they do not have to spin a drive platter or move drive heads. Instead, they can read data almost instantly. Additionally, hard drive magnetic platters are very fragile. Jarring movements and being dropped can damage the drive.

An SSD has fewer moving parts, which means fewer pieces can be damaged if it's dropped.

This makes SSDs generally more reliable. However, solid state drives do have a limited life cycle. Eventually, the drive becomes unusable. Still, for most people, the SSD lasts longer than the average computer or laptop.

Optical Storage

Optical storage uses laser beams to record and retrieve binary data. A laser beam makes tiny pits in concentric tracks on the surface of a disk. A laser scanner reads the flat areas and pits on the disk and converts it into electric signals. Because laser beams can be more precisely controlled and focused than magnetic heads, data can be stored in a much smaller space using optical storage as compared to magnetic storage. Optical storage can store large amounts of data, though it is often slower at retrieving data than magnetic storage. Because of its ability to store large amounts of data, optical storage is often used for applications that need a lot of storage space, such as those that use graphics, sounds, and a lot of text.

DID YOU KNOW?

The data stored on optical disks cannot be damaged or lost because of a power outage.

WORDS TO KNOW

random access memory (RAM): a very fast, temporary data storage system that computers use to hold the data they are manipulating.

solar power: energy from the sun converted to electricity.

volume: the quantity of data available today.

remote server: a computer that provides data to other computers and is located in a different physical location.

WORKING MEMORY

Sometimes, you need data for only a short time. Have you ever looked up the phone number for a pizza shop? You need to remember the numbers for only a few minutes while you call the shop to order a pizza. While you remember the phone number as you dial, you probably can't remember it a few hours later. This is an example of how your brain uses temporary, short-term memory.

DID YOU KNOW? Companies such as Google, Amazon, Apple, and Facebook rely on cloud server farms for the massive amounts of data they need to store. Server farms often consist of thousands of computers, which require a lot of power to run and keep cool! Some companies are investing in **solar power** to help generate the electricity they need on these farms.

A computer operates in a similar way. While you are using a computer, you need to access and use data quickly. That's why a computer includes many areas where data can be stored temporarily. Computers use **random access memory (RAM)**—often just called memory—to hold data temporarily. Using RAM, the computer can quickly access data, use or manipulate it, and then discard it if it is no longer needed. If the data is still needed, it can be saved in permanent storage.

Temporary data storage areas are smaller than long-term storage, but they are also faster. And unlike permanent data storage, when you turn the computer off, any data in temporary storage is lost.

A form of RAM

ONLINE DATA STORAGE

As the sheer **volume** of data grew, it became more difficult to store everything on a computer's hard drive. Depending on the amount of data, a single computer or even a computer network may not have had enough room to store all the necessary data. Storing large amounts of data was also expensive. Additionally, people wanted an easy way to back up their data, in case something happened to their computer or network. To solve all these problems, many people have turned to online data storage.

People who use online data storage do not have a physical device such as a flash drive or an external hard drive to store data.

Instead, they upload data across the internet to a **remote server**. The user does not usually own the server, but they can access it with a password and an internet connection. For a monthly fee (or sometimes for free), the storage provider takes care of all the details, such as server and data security, backing up the data, and server maintenance. This is also known as storing data "in the cloud." Do you use a Chromebook? Although you can save a small amount of data on the Chromebook, most of it is stored in the cloud.

WORDS TO KNOW

memory card: a type of storage device that is used for storing media and data files.

DATA STORAGE UNITS

The smartphone you got for your birthday holds 32 GB, but what does that mean? All data is stored in a computer in binary numbers using 0s and 1s. An individual binary digit is called a bit. A string of eight binary digits is a byte. A byte uses binary numerals to create one of 256 possible combinations, which can be a letter in a text message, a number, or a short word.

DID YOU KNOW?

Computers use magnetism to store data because even when the power is switched off, the magnetism remains—and so the stored data is safe.

When talking about data storage on computers and smartphones, we often use metric prefixes, including kilo, mega, and giga. A kilobyte (KB) of data is equal to about 1,000 bytes. Because each byte represents a letter, one kilobyte is enough data for you to send about four 250-character text messages. A megabyte (MB) equals about 1,000 kilobytes. And a gigabyte (GB) equals about 1,000 megabytes. Most consumer electronics, such as smartphones, tablets, hard drives, **memory cards**, and more, measure how much data they can store in gigabytes.

1 Byte = 8 Bits

1	0	1	0	0	1	0	1
1 Bit	1 Bit	1 Bit	1 Bit	1 Bit	1 Bit	1 Bit	1 Bit

1 byte	**= 8 bits**
1 kilobyte	**= 1,024 bytes**
1 megabyte	**= 1,024 kilobytes**
1 gigabyte	**= 1,024 megabytes**
1 terabyte	**= 1,024 gigabytes**

For example, a typical Blu-ray disc can hold about 25 gigabytes of data.

The largest unit of data storage—currently—is the terabyte (TB), 1 trillion bytes! Desktop computers often have a hard drive that can store two or three terabytes of data.

MANAGING STORED DATA

The more data you have, the more important it is to store it in an organized way. Is it easier to find your purple socks if they are neatly placed in an organized sock drawer or if they are thrown in a random drawer mixed with shirts and shorts? Rummaging through several drawers to hunt for the socks can take a lot of time.

In the same way, a computer that must spend a lot of time hunting for data can also experience slow performance.

Data management helps an organization figure out the best way to store and retrieve large amounts of data. At the same time, it keeps its computer systems performing at their best. Data management includes the following parts.

- Figuring out the best way to store data so it can be easily retrieved.
- Determining who can access data, and then securing data so only authorized users can access it.
- Determining how to access data without causing computer performance to suffer.
- Backing up data so it can be retrieved even if computer systems and hardware fail.
- Deciding how long to keep data.
- Creating ways and procedures to transfer data between users or software applications.
- Figuring out how advances in technology affect data management.

WORDS TO KNOW

database: a collection of data that can be easily searched.

virus: a program that enters your computer and damages or destroys stored information. Also a non-living microbe that can cause disease.

relational database: a database structured to recognize relationships among separately stored pieces of data.

database management system (DBMS): a software program that handles the storage, retrieval, and updating of data in a computer system.

ORGANIZING DATA IN A DATABASE

One way to organize and store data is to use a **database**. A database is like a big container that holds data. Just as a library stores books, a database stores data. In a library, the books are organized so you can find the one you want when you need it. In a similar way, the data in a database is organized to make it easy to find information when you need it. A database can store all types of information, including numbers, text, emails, phone records, and more.

A database is an electronic filing system. It contains fields, records, and tables. A field is a single piece of information, such as a person's phone number. A record is a complete set of fields.

Hard Drive Crash!

Nothing strikes as much fear in the heart of a computer user than the words, "My hard drive crashed!" Suddenly, all the text, pictures, music, and more that you have stored on your computer is unavailable. Instead, you can only stare at a blank computer screen. A hard drive crash occurs when a hard drive physically stops working. A fall or jolt can damage the hard drive's motors or platter. The motor that moves the hard drive may fail. The read-write heads can become uneven and scrape the platter, causing data loss. The platter itself can become warped. A **virus** or malware can make a hard drive unresponsive. Even a tiny piece of dust can damage the platter's magnetic material, causing data to be lost. Unfortunately, not all data can be recovered after a hard drive crash. That's why many people back up the important data on their computers in the cloud or on other hard drives or flash memory sticks.

For example, one record might have seven fields: a person's first name, last name, phone number, street address, city, zip code, and email address. A table is a collection of records.

DID YOU KNOW?

A database can be as simple as a single file with a list of names. A database can also be very large and include many files. Have you ever visited the doctor and had them look you up in a database?

Today, **relational databases** allow users to connect data from several tables to link to different types of information. They can also retrieve information from multiple databases. Modern databases can store different types of data, including text, numbers, audio files, pictures, and videos.

When a person wants to get data from a database, they typically use a special software program called a **database management system** (DBMS). A DBMS acts as an interface between a user and the database itself, to protect the database from being messed up by the user.

A person can use the DBMS to retrieve data from the database, edit data, and add new data to the database.

Often, the software you use for a specific purpose contains its own form of DBMS. How do you store your photos or videos on your laptop? The programs you use to create and edit your photos and videos have built-in management systems so you can easily access your files.

Data management is not hard to do when you are dealing with small amounts of data. But what happens when your database is gigantic? How does all that data stay useful and accessible for users? We'll look at big data in the next chapter!

ESSENTIAL QUESTION

What would it be like to try to use data without a data management system to help you?

Activity

WORKING WITH BINARY NUMBERS

All software, music, documents, and other data processed by a computer is stored using binary numbers. Even computer programs that carry instructions are converted into binary codes that the computer's processor can follow. And it's not just computers—all digital technologies, including DVDs, mobile phones, and satellites—use binary numbers. So, understanding binary digits is more important than ever!

To better understand how binary numbers work, you'll practice converting binary numbers into their base-10 counterparts.

➤ **To start, let's convert the binary number 1011 into a decimal number.** Use the chart below to remember the place values for each column in a binary number.

eights column	fours column	twos column	ones column	decimal number
1	0	1	1	
1 × 8 = 8	0 × 4 = 0	1 × 2 = 2	1 × 1 = 1	11

* Start with the column to the left of the "decimal number" column. It has a 1 in it. This is the ones column, so you would multiply 1 × 1 = 1.
* Move left to the next column. It also has a "1" in it. This is the twos column, so you would multiply 1 × 2 = 2
* Move left again. The fours column has a 0 in it. Multiply 0 × 4=0
* Move left to the eights column. It has a 1 in it. Multiply 1 × 8=8
* Add up all the products from each column—8 + 0 + 1 + 1 = 11—to get the decimal number. 1011 in binary is the same as number 11 in a base-10 decimal numbers.

➤ **Practice more by converting the following binary numbers to decimal numbers.** You can find the answers on page 57.

Activity

Binary number	Decimal number
1001	
10	
11	
1111	
1010	
110	
10001	
10011	

Try This!

Try converting some decimal numbers into binary numbers. Remember that each place value in a binary number increases by the power of two!

Organizing Data

Inside a computer, data is stored as many binary numbers, by magnetic, electronic, or optical systems. It can be stored in permanent and temporary locations. Computer software organizes, moves, and processes all of the binary numbers. When you turn on a computer, the basic input/output system (BIOS) gets the computer running and manages the data flow between the computer's operating system and any attached devices, such as a hard disk, keyboard, mouse, or printer. The BIOS holds simple instructions to move data in and out of different storage locations and send it for processing. The computer's operating system holds instructions to organize data into files and folders. It also manages temporary data storage and sends data to applications programs and peripheral devices like a printer. Application programs process data.

Activity

STORING COLOR AS DATA

Digital screens, from smartphones to big-screen TVs, display rich, colorful images. These devices use an RGB (red, green, blue) color system to create these intense colors. A digital screen is made up of millions of points called pixels. Each pixel contains a combination of red, green, and blue light. Think about having three light bulbs, one in each color. You can change the color of a pixel by adjusting how brightly each bulb shines. Each light bulb can go from zero (off) to 255 (all the way on). The combination of these lights and brightnesses create a color.

❯ **To see how this works, let's look at the colors white and red.** To produce a white color, all three bulbs shine brightly. To produce a red color, only the red bulb shines brightly.

Color	(Red, Green, Blue)
White	(255,255,255)
Red	(255,0,0)

❯ **In a computer, the information for each pixel's RGB combination is stored as a single, large binary number.** Colors are represented using 8-bit numbers. So, each pixel's RGB can be coded with three sets of 8 binary digits. The decimal integer 0 is 00000000 in binary, while the decimal 255 is 11111111 in binary.

For example, red (255,0,0) is represented as 11111111,00000000,00000000 in binary numbers.

❯ **Now it's your turn to code colors into data.** Using the information you learned about RGB colors, code the following colors into binary numbers. You can find the answers on page 57.

Activity

Color	(Red, Green, Blue)	Binary number
Black	(0,0,0)	
White	(255,255,255)	
Red	(255,0,0)	
Green	(0,255,0)	
Blue	(0,0,255)	
Cyan	(0,255,255)	
Magenta	(255,0,255)	
Yellow	(255,255,0)	
Gray	(128,128,128)	
Pale Yellow	(200,180,120)	

Try This!

Some computer programs code colors in hexadecimal numbers. Hexadecimal numbers have 16 numerals (instead of 10 for decimals or 2 for binary systems). They use the 10 decimal numerals (0,1,2,3,4,5,6,7,8,9) plus the first six letters of the alphabet (A,B,C,D,E,F). Research how colors are represented in hexadecimal numbers. Then, prepare a lesson to teach your classmates how to use hexadecimal numbers.

Activity

MAKE A PAPER DATABASE

A database makes it easier to find the data when you need it. You can make a database to organize your video games, DVDs, books, and more. In this activity, you'll learn how a database works by creating your own paper database.

❯ **To begin, decide what data you want to store and organize in your database.** You can use one of the following ideas or come up with your own idea.

* Your friends, their addresses, and other details
* Books you've read
* Video games you've played
* Places you have traveled

❯ **Now that you have an idea of your database topic, create a list of records for the topic.** For example, if you are making a database of books, each book would be its own record.

❯ **Next, brainstorm some fields that would be appropriate for your topic.** For example, in a database of books, you might include fields such as these.

* Title
* Author
* Publisher
* Publication date
* Date read
* Number of pages
* Genre
* Hardback or paperback
* Would you recommend the book?
* Do you own the book?
* Location

❯ **Now, write the title of each field on an index card** and tape the cards across the top of a piece of poster board.

❯ **Using additional index cards, fill out the fields for each record in your database.** Then, place the index cards under the appropriate field and place them on the poster board. Now, give the paper database to a friend or classmate. Ask them questions and have them use the database to quickly find the data they want.

Activity

Try This!

Take your paper database and enter the information into a computer spreadsheet program. What data is entered in the spreadsheet's rows? What is entered in the columns? How can you sort the data? How does putting data into a spreadsheet make it easier to find and retrieve? Was the spreadsheet you created easy to use and understand? Why or why not?

Answers to page 53

Binary number	Decimal number
1001	9
10	2
11	3
1111	15

Binary number	Decimal number
1010	10
110	6
10001	17
10011	19

Answers to page 55

Color	(Red, Green, Blue)	Binary number
Black	(0,0,0)	(00000000,00000000,00000000)
White	(255,255,255)	(11111111,11111111,11111111)
Red	(255,0,0)	(11111111,00000000,00000000)
Green	(0,255,0)	(00000000,11111111,00000000)
Blue	(0,0,255)	(00000000,00000000,11111111)
Cyan	(0,255,255)	(00000000,11111111,11111111)
Magenta	(255,0,255)	(11111111,00000000,11111111)
Yellow	(255,255,0)	(11111111,11111111,00000000)
Gray	(128,128,128)	(10000000,10000000,10000000
Pale Yellow	(200,180,120)	(11001000,10110100,01111000)

Activity

SEND A MESSAGE IN BINARY CODE

How does a computer store a text document? Instead of using letters, computers store and send text data by converting it into a series of binary digits. To understand how this works, you'll use a binary code to send a secret message to a friend!

To start, come up with a message that you want to send to one of your classmates. Keep it short! Write down the message on a piece of paper.

Using a computer with internet access, you can find the binary codes for the alphabet here.

Using these codes, convert your secret message to binary. Make sure to use the proper codes for uppercase and lowercase letters.

Once you have finished, give your friend the binary message. Have them use the same website to help convert the message from binary to text. Could your friend understand the message that you sent?

Have your friend encode a message back to you. See if you can decode the binary numbers to read the message!

Consider This!

How long did it take you to write your message in binary? What if this was the only way you could communicate with a computer or digital device?

Chapter 4

DATA GETS BIG!

There's a lot of talk in the news today about something called "big data." We know what data is—a collection of facts or statistics. But what exactly is big data? And why should we be interested in it?

Big data is more than a few pages of facts. As the name implies, big data is BIG! It's an extremely large amount of data that organizations have to deal with every day. It is typically collected and stored electronically, instead of in paper files.

Why didn't we have big data years ago? Thanks to more powerful computers, big data is the result of a dramatic increase in the ability to collect, store, and process data. Today's powerful computers have more available storage space on hard drives, flash drives, and memory cards. They can process data faster than ever because of the incredible speed of modern computer processors and internet connections.

ESSENTIAL QUESTION

How can big data put us at risk? How can it help?

WORDS TO KNOW

velocity: the rate at which data is generated and changed.

variety: the number of different data sources and types of data.

New technologies have introduced a huge number of devices that are connected to the internet, from smartphones and laptops to traffic cameras and car navigation systems. As a result, people around the world are generating and collecting more types of data faster than ever before.

VOLUME, VELOCITY, AND VARIETY

Some people use the three Vs—volume, **velocity**, and **variety**—to define big data. The three Vs make big data different from data collected in the past.

- Volume represents the sheer quantity of data available today.
- Velocity is the rate at which data is generated and changed.
- Variety is the number of different sources and types of data.

While the three Vs can help define big data, what counts as big data really depends on the person using it. A file with 10,000 data entries might be considered big data by a company with only a few employees. Yet a large corporation might not see that same file as big. Similarly, something that is considered big today might be considered tiny five years from now when technology advances have made computers even more powerful.

Recommended for You!

Have you ever seen "recommended" songs on iTunes or movies on Netflix? How do these services know what songs and movies you might like? To do this, these companies collect data from all their users' transactions and use this data to make recommendations. For example, if people who buy a lot of the same songs as you give a new song a high rating, iTunes might recommend that song to you.

WHERE DOES BIG DATA COME FROM?

Big data comes from everywhere! When you go online and shop, you create data about your interests, purchases, and web-browsing habits for internet companies and online retailers. Do you have a social media account? Anything you post, like, or follow can become a piece of big data. When an organization keeps records, from employee files to sales records, the records are sources of big data.

Data can also come from sensors embedded in a device. Today, many devices have sensors that track different types of data. Medical devices, road cameras, satellites, automobiles, cable boxes, and household appliances all collect data on the world around them. Do you wear a fitness tracker on your wrist? It's collecting big data about your steps, activity, calories burned, and sleep cycles. Other sources of big data include social media sites, business applications, and media such as podcasts, live streams, video, and audio.

Do you ever post on social media? Companies might be tracking your data.

credit: Blogtrepreneur (CC BY 2.0)

WHAT TO DO WITH BIG DATA?

While identifying the sources of big data is important, knowing what to do with all this data is critical. A big bucket of data doesn't do anyone any good if no one knows what to do with it!

Have your ever cleaned your room by throwing everything into the closet and shutting the door? How did that work out when you wanted to find a special T-shirt or book? You probably put a lot of stuff in the closet that you didn't really want or need. And by cluttering it up, you made it harder to find and use the things that you really wanted.

In the same way, organizations that use big data need to plan what they are going to do with the data.

What data is useful? What data is not needed? How are we going to store it? How are we going to access it? What are we going to use it for? What can we learn from the data? By answering questions such as these, organizations can most efficiently organize their data and put it to use.

Let's look at an example of how big data can be used in everyday life. In a big city, millions of people take public transportation, such as a bus, commuter train, or subway, to get around. The city's bus, train, and subway lines offer millions of data points—the numbers of riders, routes, times, and more. Some buses might be crowded at certain times, while others have only a few riders.

By collecting and analyzing rider data, the city government can create valuable information that helps them plan out the best public transportation schedules and routes. They can better schedule their buses, trains, and subways to meet rider needs. This is an example of how big data can be used to benefit people.

WHY IS BIG DATA IMPORTANT?

It's not the amount of big data that makes it important. It's what an organization does with it and learns from it. Data in its raw form isn't very useful, but when an organization can process and analyze that data, it can learn a lot.

When organizations analyze data, they can obtain information that helps them make smarter decisions. They can find ways of becoming more efficient. They can figure out what products and services customers want. In factories, analyzing data from machines can help factory workers identify problems and fix them almost as soon as they occur.

For example, cell phone companies collect data on the text messages and phone calls sent by millions of customers. By analyzing this data, they can determine the best places to put their cell towers, so their network can handle the volume of texts and calls without a problem.

Using Data to Fight Addiction

Across the United States, opioid addictions are ruining millions of lives. At the University of Pittsburgh, researchers are using big data to learn more about the opioid epidemic and how it spreads so they can develop solutions to fight the drug addiction. Pitt researchers are developing computer models that test how effective drug policies will be before they are implemented. The Pitt algorithm uses a variety of data sources to track the drug epidemic's past and present and predict its future. Then, the researchers use the model to simulate whether a policy will drive down overdoses and overdose deaths. Potential policies include legalizing marijuana or making naloxone, an opioid overdose medication, more widely available. They hope that this information will help officials make smarter decisions about how to fight opioid addiction.

WORDS TO KNOW

fraud: the crime of using dishonest methods to take something valuable away from someone else.

data analytics: the process of examining data to draw conclusions about it.

WHO USES BIG DATA?

Organizations in almost every industry can use big data. Big data can help organizations from banking and education to health care and retail make better decisions. Banks use big data to minimize risk and detect **fraud**. Health professionals use big data to identify trends and information that can help them better care for patients and treat disease. Manufacturing companies use big data to make products more efficiently and reduce costs.

DID YOU KNOW?

Video game companies such as Electronic Arts use big data collected from real-life sports games to predict the result of their video games.

Schools use big data to identify at-risk students and get them the help they need. Purdue University provides one example of how universities can use big data to increase the success rate of students. This university tracks student performance in different classes to identify students with low performance. The system sends alerts that warn students about potential education pitfalls they might encounter at the university.

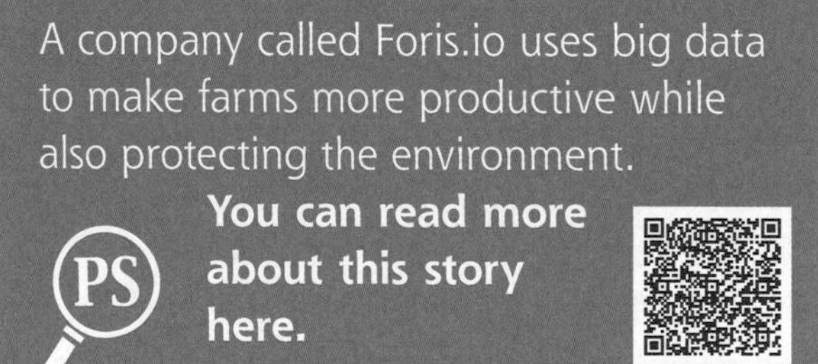
A company called Foris.io uses big data to make farms more productive while also protecting the environment.
You can read more about this story here.
Foris.io big data farms

Organizations such as the National Weather Service also use big data. The National Weather Service collects weather data from a variety of sources, such as thermometers, barometers, rain gauges, radar towers, and satellite images from around the country. Using this data, scientists create weather forecasts. They also use this data to analyze the earth's climate.

By analyzing data from as far back as the 1800s, scientists have shown that human activity has had an impact on climate change.

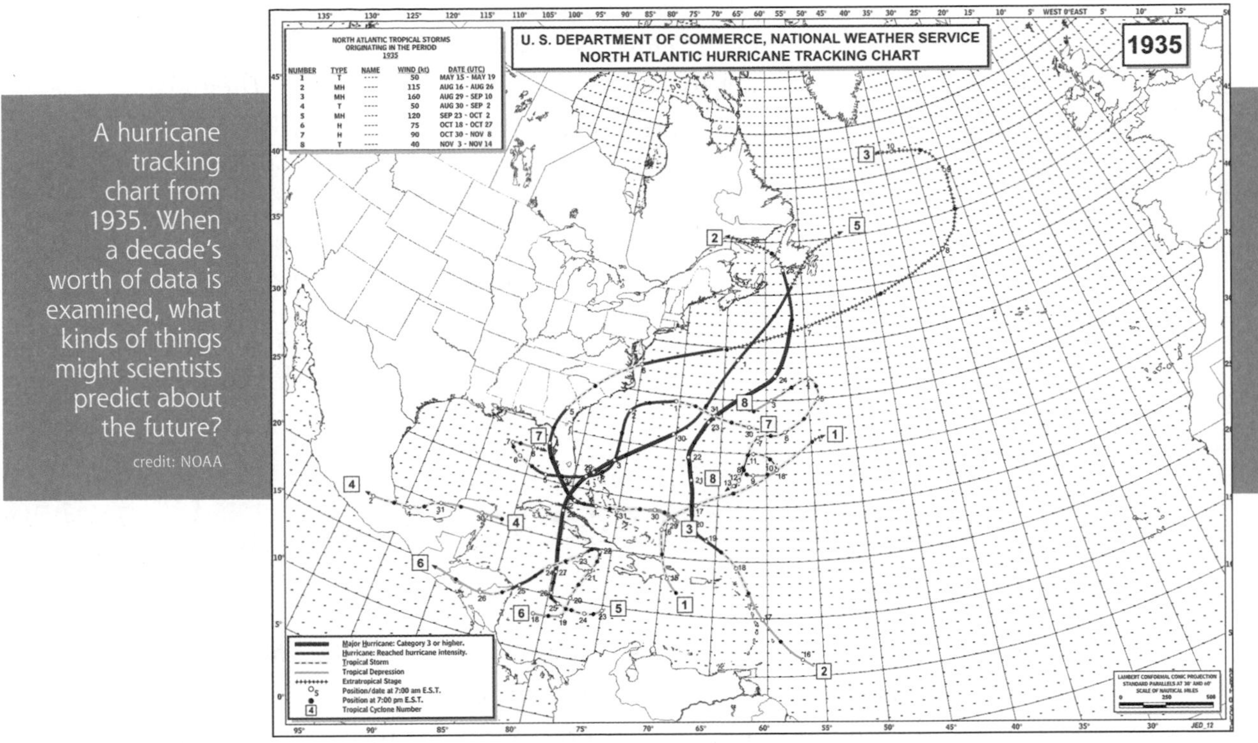

A hurricane tracking chart from 1935. When a decade's worth of data is examined, what kinds of things might scientists predict about the future?

credit: NOAA

Retail companies use big data to better understand their customers. What do customers like and what do they not like? What type of marketing works best to attract new customers? What new products do customers want? All these questions can be answered with information from big data. **Data analytics** is the process researchers use to find useful meaning in raw data. For example, the government also uses big data. Government workers can learn a lot by analyzing big data from utilities, agencies, and public works. This information can help them make better decisions about dealing with a variety of issues, from traffic jams to crime.

United Parcel Service (UPS) is an example of an organization that uses big data to improve its operations. Every day, UPS generates a lot of data, much of which comes from sensors in its nearly 100,000 delivery vehicles.

WORDS TO KNOW

targeted: directed at a group.

The sensors gather data about each vehicle's performance and driving routes. UPS used this data to redesign their drivers' routes. They also used online map data to redesign UPS driver pickups and drop-offs. The new routes made the UPS drivers more efficient. They were able to deliver more packages, faster.

The redesigned routes eliminated 85 million miles for the UPS drivers each day! This led to savings of more than 8.5 million gallons of fuel, which saved the company a lot of money and was better for the environment.

BIG DATA AND SOCIAL MEDIA

Every day, social media generates endless streams of data. Data flows from sites such as Facebook, Instagram, Snapchat, Twitter, and Pinterest. Every tweet, like, video, photograph, follow, and post on social media creates data. All this data is changing how organizations interact with and market to customers in a pretty big way.

In the past, organizations lumped customers into certain groups by age and where they lived, or whether they were married or single. Then, they created marketing campaigns for each group.

Yet, that approach wasn't very successful.

Does everyone in your class like chocolate ice cream? Probably not. Some might like vanilla, while others might not like ice cream at all—but they love cookies. An ad or promotion for chocolate ice cream probably won't work for everyone in the class.

DID YOU KNOW?

The National Football League's Atlanta Falcons use GPS technology to collect data about the movements of players during practice. The team uses this data to analyze movement and create more efficient plays.

By analyzing data from social media and other sources, organizations are getting better at identifying what people really like. Then, they can group them according to shared likes and behaviors and send them ads and promotions **targeted** for their wants and needs. In your class, using big data might create a group of chocolate ice cream lovers, vanilla ice cream lovers, and cookie lovers. Companies could send targeted ads to each group.

Have you ever looked at new bikes online? The next time you went online or on social media, did you notice anything about the ads that popped up on the sites you visited? It's likely that there were some ads for bikes, just like the ones you were looking at earlier. That's an example of how organizations are tracking what you do online to personalize their marketing specifically for you.

For example, the department store Macy's collects social media data about customer preferences and interests. It uses analytics systems to measure the positive and negative comments that customers make on social media about specific products. They use this data to forecast trends about what their customers will like. Macy's analyzed big data to figure out that people who tweeted about "jackets" also frequently used the terms "Michael Kors" and "Louis Vuitton." This information helped the retailer decide which brands of jackets to put on sale to attract customers.

WORDS TO KNOW

influenza: a highly infectious disease that causes fever, sore throat, muscle aches, and fatigue.

pandemic: a worldwide spread of disease.

vaccine: medicine designed to keep a person from getting a particular disease, usually given by needle.

coordinate: to bring different parts of a system or process together.

BIG DATA AND HEALTH CARE

In April 2009, doctors tested a 10-year-old boy for **influenza**. Test results confirmed that the patient was infected with the flu. Yet, this version of the virus was one never seen before in humans.

Two days later, a U.S. Centers for Disease Control and Prevention (CDC) laboratory confirmed a second infection with the same virus in another patient, an eight-year-old boy who lived 130 miles away from the first boy to fall sick. The two patients had no known connection. Lab analysis at the CDC found the flu viruses in these patients were very similar, and different from any other flu virus seen before.

Immediately, the CDC opened an investigation into the new influenza virus they called H1N1.

The new H1N1 virus, also called swine flu, spread quickly. Within weeks, public health agencies worldwide feared a **pandemic** had begun. Because the H1N1 virus was so new, there were no readily available **vaccines** to prevent it. Instead, public health officials had to find a way to slow its spread.

DID YOU KNOW? The H1N1 influenza virus was originally called "swine flu". Laboratory tests showed that the virus was similar to influenza viruses known to affect pigs.

To slow the spread of H1N1, doctors first needed to know where it already was. In the United States, the CDC asked doctors, health clinics, and hospitals across the country to notify them when any new patients were diagnosed with H1N1.

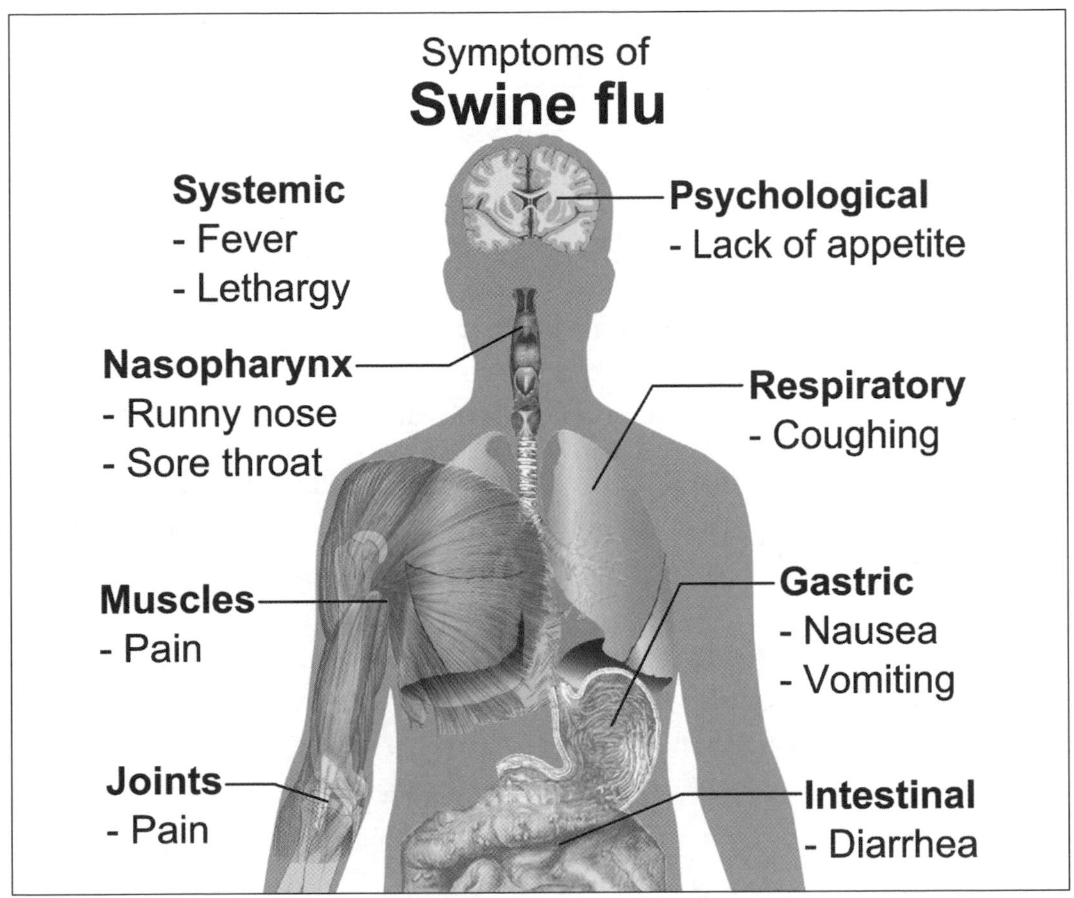

A poster showing the symptoms of H1N1

The CDC used this information to build models that could predict where, when, and how frequently cases of H1N1 would appear. With this information, the CDC and local communities could better **coordinate** emergency medical responses. They could also make sure enough vaccine was produced and sent to the places where it was needed.

Yet, by the time scientists at the CDC got the information, it was already a week or two old. With a virus that spread so quickly, the CDC was being forced to make decisions without the data it needed. It needed better data more quickly to stop the spread of this disease.

WORDS TO KNOW

search query: a question or query that a person enters into an internet search engine.

keyword: a word or phrase that describes online content.

correlation: a connection between two things.

accuracy: free from mistake or error.

Meanwhile, engineers at Google had already been working on a way to predict the spread of the flu that coming winter. They wanted to predict flu cases not just nationally, but also regionally and even state by state.

Owners of one of the biggest internet search engines, Google had access to the records of 3 billion **search queries** made on its site each day. And because it saved them all, the company had a lot of data ready to use.

Google engineers created a flu-predicting algorithm based on the idea that people who are feeling sick enter phrases such as "flu symptoms" and "fever" into a search engine before they call their doctor.

These researchers believed they could use this data to create an early warning system to predict the spread of flu outbreaks.

For example, if Google engineers noticed an increase in search queries with the words "fever" and "sore throat" in Baltimore, Maryland, they might predict an increase in the number of flu cases in that city during the next few weeks.

To build the algorithm, Google engineers tested a number of **keywords** and phrases related to the flu. They compared these search terms to CDC flu data from 2003 to 2008. They found a strong **correlation**, or connection, between certain search terms and the spread of flu. Using the search data and model, they could predict the spread of the flu, and they could do it almost in real time, not a week or two later.

When H1N1 struck in 2009, Google's method of using search engine data to predict the spread of the virus proved to be very useful. It was faster than the CDC's predictive models. The Google flu tracker could be updated daily and could provide close to real-time estimates and predictions. Health officials could use it as an early warning system.

Pitfalls of Big Data

When Google's flu-tracking service was launched, reports stated it predicted flu cases with 97-percent **accuracy** compared to CDC data. However, later reports showed this wasn't quite true. During the 2012–13 flu season, the Google flu-tracking technology greatly overestimated the number of flu cases in the United States. The extra media attention on the flu might have made more people search symptoms online. Also, Google engineers discovered that their model was gathering search queries about other health conditions that used similar search terms, not just the flu. In 2015, Google shut down its flu-tracking website. Now, it passes search query data to health organizations to use in their own models.

Look at data for previous years at this website. Do the numbers make sense to you? The amount of data makes it difficult for humans to read, which is why computers are useful!

Google flu track

WORDS TO KNOW

ethical: doing the right thing.

structured data: data that is organized in a pre-determined way, such as a field in a database record.

unstructured data: data that is not organized in a predetermined way, such as a photograph.

PRIVACY AND SECURITY

Today, almost everything you do online, and even offline, can be tracked. Imagine you're at a store at the mall. You wander around the store, stopping to look at some shirts, sweaters, and jeans before deciding to buy a blue shirt. You leave the store with the purchase and go home. What you might not realize is that some retailers can track how much time you spent in each section of the store and the path you followed. The retailer uses the data to develop better products, services, and store layouts.

This example illustrates one of the **ethical** concerns with big data. Today, data about consumers is constantly being generated, flowing from mobile devices, sensors in everyday items, online activity, and more. This data helps companies understand their customers and their behavior better than ever before, which can benefit everyone. But, this increased knowledge comes with a threat to privacy.

Protecting Consumers in the European Union

Some countries are putting rules in place to govern data privacy and security. In the European Union, the General Data Protection Regulation took effect in May 2018. It requires companies to make sure consumers give clear consent to having their personal data collect. It also requires companies to make sure consumers understand how their data will be used. Consumers who do not want to have their data collected can opt out and request that companies erase all of their personal data.

In 2016, a group of Danish researchers publicly released data from nearly 70,000 users of an online dating website called OkCupid. The data included the answers to thousands of profile questions asked by the site. It also included usernames, ages, genders, locations, and personality traits.

DID YOU KNOW? **Structured data** is organized in a predetermined way. An example of structured data is a field in a database record or table. **Unstructured data** is not organized in a predetermined way. An example of unstructured data is an email or a photograph.

When they answered the profile questions, the website users did not know their information would be made public.

As more organizations jump on the big-data bandwagon, questions have risen about the ethics of big data. Who owns the data being analyzed? When does the use of this data cross the line into misuse? What privacy can people expect online or in their homes? People need to decide what data they are willing to share. And organizations need to be clear about how they are using the data, so people can make informed decisions.

Businesses track the paths people take when shopping in a store or mall, and use that information to make decisions about what products get displayed where.

WORDS TO KNOW

hacker: an expert at programming and solving problems on a computer. Also describes someone who illegally gains access to and sometimes tampers with information in a computer system.

malicious: intending to do harm.

Closely related to privacy is the issue of data security. As more data is stored electronically, the risk of it being stolen or used without permission is increasing. What happens when a **hacker** accesses data without permission? Some hackers are simply curious. They want to understand how a computer network operates. Other hackers have **malicious** intentions. They break into computer networks to steal valuable data that they can sell for profit.

How can you keep your information safe online? Always follow these tips!

- Check your settings on social media platforms to ensure you are as private as possible.
- Never share passwords, a Social Security number, address, or last name with others.
- Limit what you post about. Don't post anything you wouldn't want your grandmother or a future boss to see!

DID YOU KNOW?

In the United States, no single federal law regulates the collection, use, and sharing of personal data. Instead, several federal and state laws and regulations apply to specific types of data, such as financial or health data.

In recent years, a growing number of data breaches have occurred in organizations around the world. Hackers have stolen personal data that organizations have stored, including customers' Social Security numbers, passwords, financial information, and more. In 2017, the consumer credit reporting agency Equifax announced that the personal data of 143 million Americans—nearly half of the country's population—had been stolen. Why is this such a problem?

Big data is here to stay. It will continue to grow and evolve. But capturing big data is not enough. We also need to understand it. In the next chapter, we'll take a deeper look at how people are working to better understand data.

ESSENTIAL QUESTION

How can big data put us at risk? How can it help?

Activity

PRIVACY VS. CONVENIENCE

Every time you go shopping online and in person, you create data that companies can use to learn more about what you need and want to buy. Among other things, this information allows companies to design specific promotions geared toward your interests. But at what point does data-gathering become an invasion of privacy?

What do you think the balance should be between privacy and the benefits of big data? Start by brainstorming a list of pros and cons for big data, including its usefulness and its impact on privacy. Create a chart to visually show your information.

Choose a side—do you think companies should be able to use big data in any way they see fit? Or do you think privacy rights are more important and should be protected, even if it means big data cannot be used to its fullest? Write a persuasive paragraph supporting your position and share it with your class.

Many Americans are not happy with the lack of control they have over the data companies collect about them online. **You can read more about it in a report from the Annenberg School for Communication at the University of Pennsylvania here.**

PS

UPenn data tradeoff

Consider This!

Do you think privacy protection rules or laws should be passed to regulate how big data is used? Explain your position.

Activity

FINDING BIG DATA

Big data is all around us. Devices, machines, websites, organizations, and more are tracking data every second. Yet, sometimes it can be difficult to find data. And once found, what can you use the data for? A lot of data is raw—unprocessed and unorganized. This can make it difficult to figure out where it came from and how it can best be used. In this activity, you'll explore a website or two and evaluate the data it offers.

➤ To start, with an adult's permission, choose a website to explore from these examples.

1. Web archive

2. Wind Sensor network

3. Twitter sentiment

5. Alternative Fuel Locator

DID YOU KNOW?

According to the website Statista, 85 percent of the digital photos taken in 2017 will be shot with a smartphone. Only 10.3 percent will be taken with digital cameras. What do you think will be the next version of a phone camera? Watch cameras? Jewelry cameras? Clothing cameras? What would you like to see?

Activity

As you explore your chosen website, answer the following questions.

* What kind of data does this website have?
* How does the website present its data? Is this format helpful? Does it help you understand the data better? How do you think it could be improved?
* Is the data live or static?
* What is data on this website potentially useful for? How can the data and information provided be used?
* Where does the data on this website come from? Is it a reputable source? Why or why not?
* Do you think this is an example of big data? Why or why not?

Try This!

What limits (if any) should be placed on the use of this data? Are there any privacy or security issues related to using this data?

Using Big Data in Sports

In recent years, the use of data in sports is growing in popularity. Data analytics examines large amounts of data and statistics about players to determine patterns and make predictions about future performance. Most major professional sports teams have data analytics experts, sometimes even an entire department. Using data analysis, teams can use information to determine whether to bench a player or play him, where to place defensive players on the field, whether to draft a player, sign a free agent, or trade for one. However, data analytics are not foolproof. Recognizing this, most teams that use data analytics do not rely on them exclusively. Instead, information from data analytics becomes one part of the decision-making process.

Activity

USING BIG DATA TO TARGET CUSTOMERS

Companies use big data to build profiles about their customers, which helps them design more effective marketing campaigns and promotions. This information can include purchase history, race, occupation, age, relationship status, reading habits, credit history, and even online conversations. In this activity, you'll explore how using big data to target customers can improve sales and reduce marketing costs for companies.

❯ **To start, you'll be the marketing director for a company that sells three products—harmonicas, basketballs, and drawing kits.** How can you sell the most products while reducing the amount of money you spend on marketing?

❯ **Create a marketing flyer for each of your products.** Hand out the flyers randomly to your class, so each student receives one. Some will receive the harmonica flyer, while others will receive the basketball or drawing kit promotions.

❯ **Of the people who received a harmonica flyer, how many will buy one?** Ask your customers. For those who received the basketball flyer, how many will buy? What about for the drawing kits? Record the sales data.

❯ **Gather some data about the students in your class.** Divide them into groups according to hobbies—sports, art, and music. Now, resend your marketing flyers, but this time target your customers by interest. How many students will make a purchase now? Record the sales data.

❯ **What happened to sales when you used data about the students to target your marketing?** Create a chart to visually present your results.

Consider This!

What other types of data might help you divide your student customers into even more specific groups? How could this be used to increase sales or reduce costs?

Activity

INTERPRETING BIG DATA

Organizations use big data to help them make better decisions. In this activity, you'll explore how big data can be used for insight into customer behavior.

Imagine that you work for a cable and internet provider. You want to better understand your customers' needs so that you can plan programming and sell commercial time to advertisers. Your marketing department has conducted a survey of recent customers about their viewing habits. Here's what they report.

Question: How many hours did you spend watching television this week?	
Responses from 15 women	**Responses from 15 men**
4, 2, 8, 15, 20, 1, 5, 6, 9, 12, 7, 3, 4, 10, 8	10, 12, 15, 8, 5, 17, 24, 18, 3, 9, 11, 20, 10, 14, 15

Question: What type of television programming do you typically watch?	
Responses from 15 women	**Responses from 15 men**
Drama—6 Sitcom—4 Reality—2 Sports—3	Drama—2 Sitcom—4 Reality—1 Sports—8

Analyze the data by answering the following questions.

* Calculate the mean number of hours the women spent watching television this week. The mean is the average of all the numbers. To calculate it, add up all the numbers and divide the sum by the number of responses.
* Calculate the mean number of hours the men spent watching television.
* What are the top two most popular types of programs for women? For men?
* What does this information tell you about the viewing habits of men vs. women? How can you use this information to make programming decisions?

Consider This!

Is interpreting data according to gender or race a form of **stereotyping**? Why or why not?

WORDS TO KNOW

stereotype: the inaccurate belief that all people who share a single physical or cultural trait are the same.

Chapter 5

UNDERSTANDING DATA

Now that companies and governments have lots and lots of data, and they know what they want to do with it, how do they go about putting it into a form they can understand? After all, most of us don't know how to read binary numbers.

Collecting massive amounts of data is just the first step. In order for data to be useful, it must also be understood. There are several techniques people use to better understand the data they have collected.

ESSENTIAL QUESTION

Why is data easier to understand when it's in a visual format?

VISUALIZE IT

WORDS TO KNOW

visualization: to put something in a picture or other visual format.

interactive: having a two-way flow of information between a computer and a user.

Do you find it easier to understand something if you can see it? **Visualization** is the easiest way for our brains to receive and process large amounts of data. Maybe it's a graph of results from your chemistry lab or a pie chart that shows how you spent your allowance. Looking at the data visually can help you quickly see where you're spending your money. Just a glance reveals that you're spending too much money on milkshakes after school. This information can help you make better choices about how you spend your allowance, so that you can save for the new pair of rollerblades that you really want.

In the same way, organizations that collect a lot of data use visualization techniques to help them understand it. Data visualization is any way of putting data into a visual format to make it clearer. A visual format can be a picture, graph, or chart. Looking at the data this way helps us to quickly spot patterns, trends, and correlations.

DID YOU KNOW? A heat map is a two-dimensional representation of data in which values are represented by colors.

Data visualization tools can be simple or complex.

A simple bar chart or line graph can clearly display data. Data can also be displayed using infographics, geographic maps, heat maps, and more.

Some visual images can even be **interactive**. Users can click on parts of the image to learn more about the data. Visuals can also include tools that alert users when the data has been updated or when certain conditions are met. Do your parents get alerts from their bank about how much money they have in their account? That's a result of data!

DATA ANALYTICS

Data visualization is one way to understand large amounts of data. Data analytics is another way. Data analytics is the process of examining raw data to draw conclusions about it. People have been working to analyze data for years. In the 1950s, businesses manually studied data to identify trends and patterns. Today, the speed and efficiency of computers and other technologies allow organizations to analyze data much faster.

Businesses can identify patterns and relationships in data and use that information to help them make immediate decisions.

Imagine that you own a business that sells pet care products. You realize that you need a faster and more efficient way of designing new products. If you could quickly analyze the pet care data your employees gather, your business could more efficiently create new pet care products. To solve this problem, you turn to data analytics.

Data analytics allows you to sort through a mountain of data to come to a conclusion. For example, if you want to understand what types of products your customers buy, you might create a table to help you visualize your sales. Using a data analytics tool, you can sort that data by location, type of pet, type of product, and more. With this information, you can quickly see what types of products your customers like to buy.

Often, organizations use special computer systems and software to analyze large sets of data. Typically, data used for analytics is either historical records of past events or new information that can be analyzed in real-time.

DID YOU KNOW? Online retailers use powerful tools to constantly analyze the prices their competitors charge for the same products. Then, they lower or raise their own prices to increase sales and profits.

No matter what type of data is used or what type of analysis is done, the overall goal is the same—to find patterns, correlations, and other information that can help an organization make better decisions.

WHAT'S SO IMPORTANT ABOUT DATA ANALYTICS?

What good is having a lot of data, if you can't use it? Data analytics helps organizations make sense of their data and use it to make better decisions. This leads to more sales, reduced costs, more efficient operations, and more satisfied employees and customers.

In many industries, keeping customers satisfied is critical. But sometimes, it's hard to measure how happy customers are. Businesses might not find out until weeks later that a customer was not satisfied with a purchase.

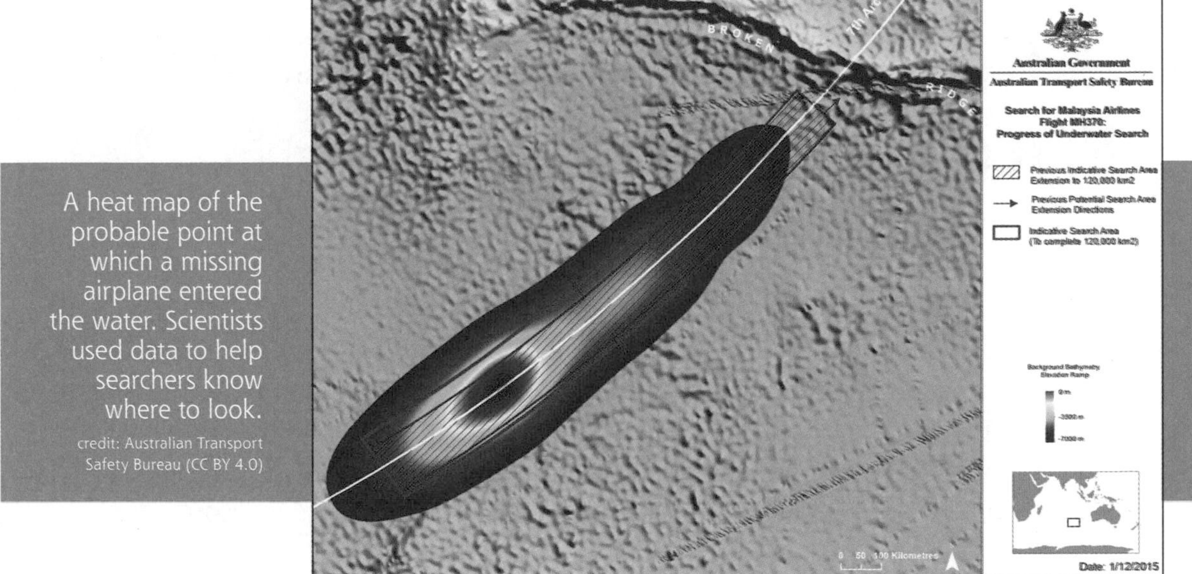

A heat map of the probable point at which a missing airplane entered the water. Scientists used data to help searchers know where to look.

credit: Australian Transport Safety Bureau (CC BY 4.0)

Using data analytics, companies can use customer data to immediately identify problems, while there's still time to fix them.

For Lenovo, the world's largest manufacturer of PCs and tablets, data analytics helped keep important customers satisfied. Lenovo was designing a new keyboard layout on one of its bestselling personal computers. The company's corporate analytics unit, whose job it was to use a variety of data to make better business decisions, was searching through online text data that included mentions of Lenovo.

The analytics unit discovered an online forum where a Lenovo customer had written an extremely favorable review of the existing computer design, including the keyboard. The review had gathered 2,000 comments from other forum users and Lenovo customers.

Lenovo realized that this small, but significant group of customers—freelance software developers and gamers—were very satisfied with the current keyboard design. A changed keyboard could have resulted in some very unhappy customers, who may have taken their business to other computer manufacturers!

Try It On!

In today's digital world, shoppers no longer go to a store, try on a few outfits, and pick the one they like the best. Now, they might browse a store's website and find the clothing they like. Chico's, a women's clothing retailer, uses data analytics to connect customers with the clothes they want. With data analytics, Chico's can better understand what products customers want, what drives them to buy, and what is the best way to contact customers. Instead of mailing every promotion to every customer, through data analytics the company can decide which people to contact. This helps keep marketing costs down. It also means better communications with customers.

This information was not something that had been discovered by traditional design reviews. Lenovo scrapped its keyboard redesign and avoided a potentially costly mistake.

DID YOU KNOW?

A data warehouse is a large store of data from a variety of sources within a company.

DATA-ANALYTICS PROCESS

Data analytics involves many steps. Especially in complex or large projects, much of the work occurs in the beginning—collecting, organizing, and preparing data. Then, analytical models must be developed, tested, and revised to make sure they work properly. Teams of people work on these projects, including data analysts and data engineers.

First, data scientists decide what data they need for their analytics project. They work with data engineers and other information technology staff to collect the necessary data. Because raw data might come from different sources, it is often in different formats. Data scientists and engineers work to combine and edit the data, so it is all in the same format. Then, it can be loaded into a data-analytics tool, such as a database or data warehouse.

WORDS TO KNOW

predictive modeling: a process that uses data mining and probability to forecast outcomes.

data mining: the use of models to automatically search through large amounts of data.

machine learning: a field of computer science that teaches a computer to perform a task by giving it a set of examples.

Once the data is ready, data scientists and engineers clean the data. They search for and fix any quality problems that could affect the analytics. For example, they may run special programs to search for and delete duplicate entries. They also organize the data for use in analytics tools.

Then, data scientists build an analytical model. They might use **predictive modeling** tools or other software. To test the model, the data scientists often run it using a partial set of data. Then, they revise and retest the model. This testing and revising continues until the model operates properly. Finally, the data scientists run the model using the full data set. The model produces information the organization can use.

The last step in the data-analytics process is communicating the results to an organization's decision-makers. This is often done with data visualization techniques.

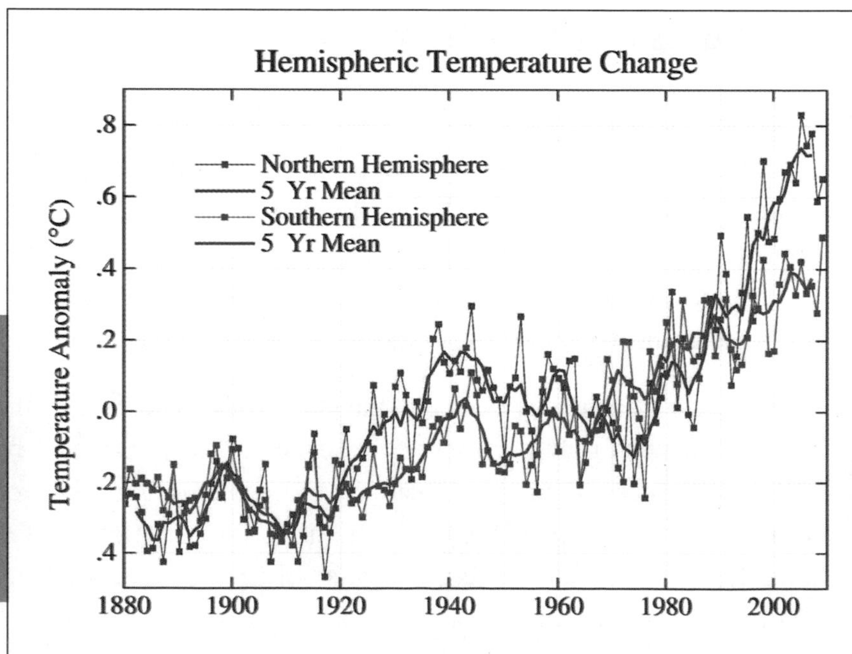

A line graph showing temperature during a long span of time. This kind of graph is useful for comparing conditions across many years.

credit: NASA GISTEMP

Data-analytics teams can create charts, graphs, and other infographics to make the results of their analytical models easy to understand. As new data becomes available, the analytical models can be rerun and the results updated.

DID YOU KNOW?

One of the main goals of data analytics is to find a correlation, a relationship, or a connection between two things.

DATA MINING

Organizations use several tools and technologies to help them gather, organize, and analyze their data. One common tool is **data mining**. Data mining uses models to automatically search through large amounts of data. It uses mathematical algorithms to segment data, discover patterns and trends, and predict likely future outcomes.

Text Mining

More and more, data exists in the form of text, including comments on social media sites, user forums, and other places. With text-mining technology, users can analyze text data from online and offline sources. Text mining uses **machine learning** and other technologies to search through emails, blogs, social media sites, surveys, and more to analyze large amounts of text data. It can identify areas of importance for an organization. For example, if many users are posting online about a problem with a company's product, text mining can promptly identify the increased online chatter and identify the problem. With this information, the company can quickly fix the problem and send out messages to customers and the public about its fix before customer relationships are damaged.

WORDS TO KNOW

web analytics: software programs that track, collect, analyze, and report data about website traffic.

Organizations often use data mining to help them understand customer data. Data-mining models can analyze customer data for patterns, groupings, or other indicators that help them make better marketing decisions. Data-mining models can also look at data about a manufacturing plant's downtime to help managers improve production processes.

DID YOU KNOW?

Today, the quantity of data that moves across the internet EVERY SECOND is greater than ALL the data stored on the internet only 20 years ago, according to researchers MIT.

Data-mining models can even help organizations hire employees that are a good fit. Some organizations gather data about their best employees from social media accounts. They use this data to build models that they can use to analyze job candidates to predict if they will be a good fit with the organization. Think about this the next time you post something to social media!

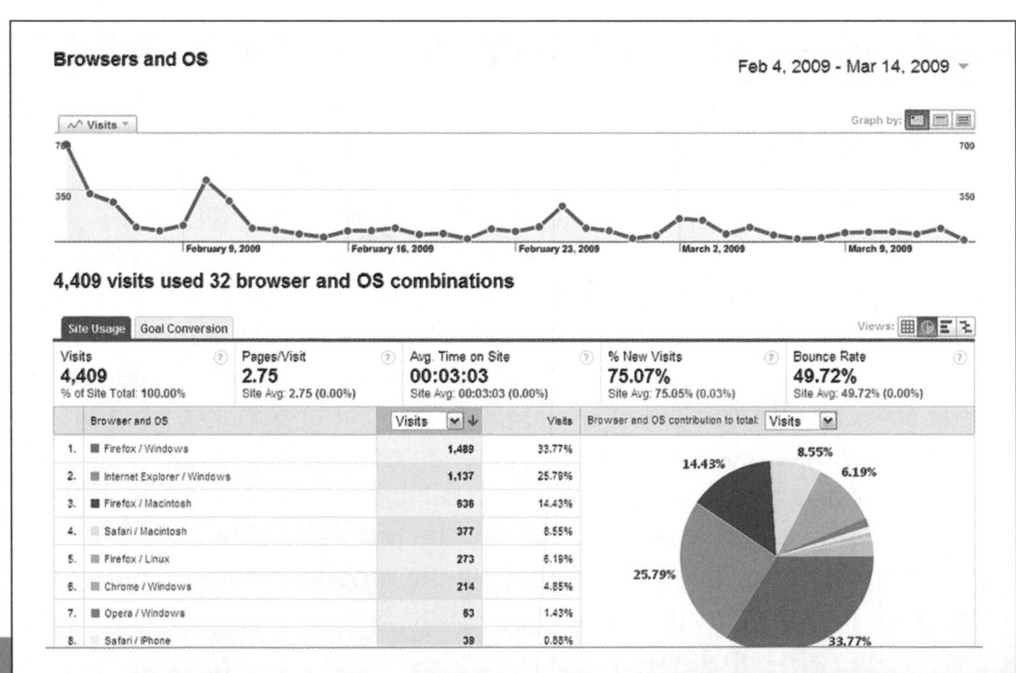

This is the kind of information you might see when you analyze how a web page is performing.

WEB ANALYTICS

Organizations can learn a lot about people from their behavior online. What websites does a person visit? What sites did they come from? How long do they stay on each site? What pages do they visit? What products or information do they click on? Do they make any purchases? How do they interact with others online? These are just a few types of data that can be collected about a person online. Does this make you wonder how the information you post online is being used?

Web analytics track, collect, analyze, and report data about a visitor's behavior on a website. Companies use the information they learn from web analytics to make the web experience better for visitors, encourage customers to buy goods or services, and even increase the amount of money each customer spends.

The analysis can predict the likelihood of a customer returning for a new purchase and help a company personalize a website for repeat customers.

Web analytics can also track the number of purchases made by individuals or by groups of customers, such as customers from a certain region. It can predict which products customers are most likely to buy in the future. All this information can help companies better market to customers. It can also improve a website's effectiveness. These efforts increase sales and reduce the cost of marketing.

What does all this data mean for the future? Will companies keep gaining more and more knowledge about their customers? Is there a limit to how much data we can produce and keep? We'll look at the future of data in the next chapter!

ESSENTIAL QUESTION

Why is data easier to understand when it's in a visual format?

Activity

CHART YOUR THANKSGIVING TRADITIONS

Charts and graphs are popular ways to present data visually. In this activity, you will explore two popular types of visuals—pie charts and bar graphs—and use them to present data.

❯ **To start, take a survey of your classmates' Thanksgiving traditions.** Where does each family celebrate Thanksgiving dinner? Tell classmates they can choose one of five possible responses, including at home, relative's house, friend's house, restaurant, or other. Gather your survey responses and record the data.

❯ **Once you have all the data, you'll need to perform a few calculations.** To calculate the percentage of the total for each of the five responses, use the following formula:

(# of responses for a location ÷ all responses) × 100 = percentage of total

For example, if you received 25 responses, and 10 of them said they ate dinner at home, the formula to calculate the percentage of total for "At Home" is calculated by:

(10 ÷ 25) × 100 = 40 percent

❯ **After you have calculated the percentage for each location, the sum should equal 100 percent.** If it does not, you may have to round one or two of the answers so that they total 100.

❯ **Create a pie chart with this information.** Estimate the size of each pie sector and label it. What information does the pie chart show?

❯ **Use the same data to create a bar graph.** Compare the bar graph and the pie chart. How are they the same? How are they different? Which one does a better job of presenting the information? Explain why.

Activity

Consider This!

Think about how your pie chart and bar graph would change if you collected more data by adding more people to your survey. How does increasing your survey size affect your data? Does it make the information more or less accurate? Explain.

What Type of Graph to Use?

There are many ways to show data visually. Here are a few common graphs and their typical uses.

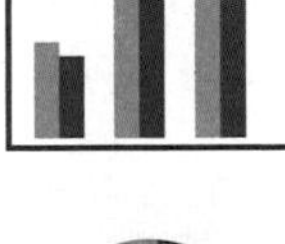

- **Bar graph:** This is typically used for big sets of data to compare data.

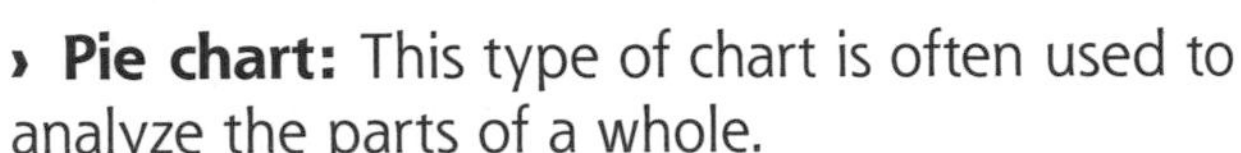

- **Pie chart:** This type of chart is often used to analyze the parts of a whole.

- **Double-line graph:** This graph is a good choice if you have two sets of data to compare.

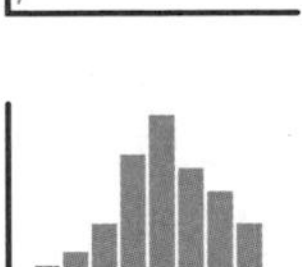

- **Histogram:** This graph is good for comparing data that falls into ranges, such as age groups.

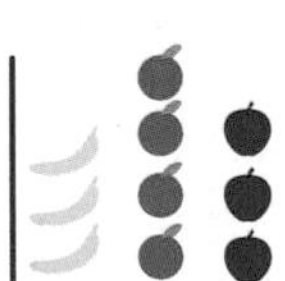

- **Pictograph:** This visual makes data fun, engaging, and informative.

- **Stem and leaf plots:** These graphs work well for data that needs to be organized by place value.

Stem	Leaf
2	5, 8, 9
3	4

Activity

COLLECT DATA FOR ANALYSIS

Why do we collect data? To learn meaningful information? What is the data trying to tell us? How can what we learn from data help us? In this activity, you will collect data and organize it so that you can derive useful information from it.

❯ **To start, brainstorm something that you want to know more about, something that you can study with data.** You can use one of the following ideas or come up with one of your own.

* What type of wildlife is the most common in your neighborhood?
* Do more people own cats or dogs in your neighborhood?
* What is the average family size for the students in your class?
* What is the average height of the students in your class? How does that compare to other classes in your school?
* What is this year's average temperature in your area? How does that compare to the average from another year?

❯ **Next, you'll have to collect data.** Some data is collected automatically on the internet or via computers and other electronic devices. Other times, data is collected through other methods, such as the following.

* **Observations**. This type of data collection involves watching someone or something. For example, a person might observe how many people walk dogs down a street.
* **Interviews**. This type of data collection centers on talking to others. Interviewers often ask several questions and collect the person's answers as data. For example, they might interview residents on a street about their pets.
* **Surveys**. A survey is a series of written questions. A person gives out a survey to a targeted group and then records the answers as data.
* **Measurement**. People can gather data by measuring objects.
* **Records**. People gather the measurements done and recorded by other people.

Activity

After you decide on a topic, decide what type of data you need to collect and how you will collect it. Once your plans are in place, collect the data you need.

Now that you have collected all your data, what do you do with it? To organize and analyze it, you might make charts, tables, or spreadsheets. You can also perform calculations. Do you see any relationships or patterns in your data? Do you see any trends? What does that tell you? What information have you learned from your data collection and analysis? Is it what you expected or did the data show something unexpected?

The final step is to look at the results to answer or solve a question. What did your data find, solve, and answer? How is it helpful?

To Explore More

Create a visual presentation of your data and present it to your class. What type of visual format will you choose? Explain your choice.

Other Tools

There are many tools used to analyze data. Here are just a few!

- **Hadoop:** A software tool that organizes data and gives organizations the ability to gather, store, and analyze large sets of data.
- **NoSQL:** A database tool that can be used for a wide variety of data models. NoSQL stands for "Not Only SQL" and is an alternative to traditional databases in which data sits in tables. NoSQL databases are useful when working with large sets of data across multiple computers.
- **Google Analytics:** A group of tools for collecting, consolidating, reporting, and analyzing data.

Activity

REPRESENTING DATA WITH GRAPHS

Presenting data visually often makes it easier for people to understand. One way to show data visually is through a graph. In this activity, we are going to explore several types of graphs and how they can be used to represent data.

➤ **To start, ask your classmates a question.** How many phones do they have in their home? How many televisions? How many bicycles? Choose one of these questions and record each person's answer. You'll use this data to create different types of graphs.

➤ **First, use the data to create a line plot.** A line plot is a graph that shows the frequency of data along a number line. Find the smallest and largest numbers in your data and place each at either end of a number line. Draw an X on the number line for each answer. If there are multiple answers with the same number, place the additional Xs above the previous one. How can you use this graph to find the **range** (the difference between the largest and smallest values), **mode** (the value that occurs most often), and **median** (the middle value) of the data?

➤ **A line plot works well when the range of data is not very wide.** When a data set has a wider range, a stem and leaf plot may be more useful. A stem and leaf plot is a table where each data value is split into its first digit or digits (the stem) and its last digit (the leaf). For example, the data values of 25, 28, 29, and 34 would look like this on a stem and leaf plot.

Stem	Leaf
2	5, 8, 9
3	4

➤ **Create your own stem and leaf plot by using the points scored by your favorite NFL team in each game of the 2017 season as the data.** How can you use this graph to find the range, mode, and median of the data?

WORDS TO KNOW

range: the difference between the highest and lowest values in a set of numbers.

mode: the number that appears most often in a set of numbers.

median: the middle value in a list of numbers.

Activity

❯ **Another type of graph you can use is a box and whisker plot.** This type of graph makes it easy to see how data is distributed along a number line. To create a box and whisker plot, first put it in order from least to greatest. For example:

1,3,4,7,9,10,12,14,15,27,38

❯ **Next find the median (middle number) of the data set.** In our example, the median is 10. The median is also called the second quartile.

1,3,4,7,9,10,12,14,15,27,38

❯ **Next, find the first and third quartiles,** which are the median of the numbers to the left and right of 10.

1,3,4,7,9,10,12,14,15,27,38

❯ **Then, draw a plot line.** Mark the first, second, and third quartiles on the plot line.

❯ **Make a box by drawing horizontal lines** to connect the quartiles.

❯ **Mark the outliers (the smallest and largest numbers) in the data on the plot line with a small dot.** Then connect the outliers to your box with a line. These are the whiskers on your box. With a box and whiskers plot, you can easily see the distributions of numbers in a data set.

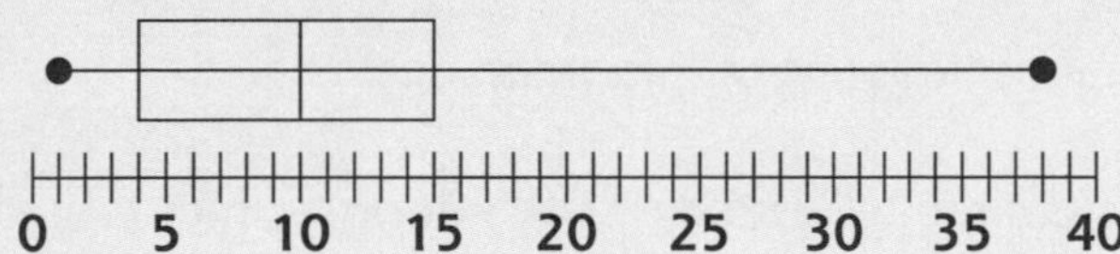

Try This!

Now that you've learned how to create a box and whiskers plot, create your own using the NFL points data that you've already gathered. How can you use this graph to find the range, mode, and median of the data?

Activity

INFO THROUGH INFOGRAPHICS

As the amount of data explodes, infographics have become an effective way to visually present data. Infographics are visual representations of data, information, or knowledge. They are designed to present data and information quickly and clearly. You can probably find an infographic on just about any topic. Look at a few of these examples.

* An analysis of the Beatles

* Volcano's Inside Out

* America's most popular birthdays

* The psychology of color in logo design

Infographics present data in a creative and informative way. They show data in a neat, colorful format that is easy to share and save.

There are several main categories of infographics.

* **Statistical:** uses data to tell a story
* **Informational:** presents text-based information
* **Timeline:** shows how data changes over time
* **Process:** provides a step-by-step procedure
* **Geographic:** presents geographic data
* **Comparison:** compares and contrasts two things
* **Hierarchical:** stacks information based on levels (like a pyramid)
* **Chart-Centric:** uses simple graphs and charts to make data stand out

Activity

Now it's your turn to make an infographic. Choose a subject that you would like to present. It might be data about the birthdays of everyone in your class, the average rainfall in your town during the past month, the steps needed to make cookies, or another topic that interests you. Gather the relevant data.

Once you have gathered the data, decide what type of infographic you will use to present it. Create your infographic either by drawing it by hand or using a computer.

DID YOU KNOW?

The human brain can process entire images that the eye sees for as little as 13 milliseconds, according to MIT researchers.

Once you have finished, present your infographic to your class. Ask your classmates what data stood out the most to them on the infographic. Did they find the infographic's format easy to understand?

To Explore More

Try presenting the same data in a different type of infographic. Share the new infographic with your classmates. Which format do they prefer? Why? Was one format more effective at sharing relevant data? Why or why not? How do you think the format of an infographic affects how people understand data?

You can learn a little more about each of these types of infographics and see examples of each at this website.

9 infographic templates

Activity

WHAT'S THE MOST POPULAR SKITTLE?

How many colors are in a bag of Skittles candy? How many of each color are in a bag? Which colors are the most common and least common? In this activity, you'll gather and analyze data to answer these questions!

❯ **To start, gather several bags of Skittles candy, all the same size.** Open one bag and sort the candies by color. Record the number of each color in a spreadsheet or table. Repeat this for each bag, recording the data each time.

❯ **After you finish collecting data, organize it so that you can answer some questions.** What color is the most common? What color is the least common?

❯ **Create a visual chart or graph to show this information.** Try a bar chart and then a pie chart. Which visual format makes it easier to answer the questions?

❯ **Now, look at your data to answer the following question: How many candies are in a bag?** What is the average number of candies across all bags? (Hint: To calculate an average, use this formula: total number of candies ÷ total number of bags = average). How does each individual bag differ from the average? Create a visual chart to show this information.

❯ **Organize your data to answer this question: Does the amount of each color change in each bag?** What is the average amount of each color in a bag? How do the individual bags differ from the average? How can you show this visually?

Consider This!

How certain do you feel about your conclusions? Would any additional data make you feel more certain about your conclusions? Explain why or why not.

Activity

EXPLORING DATA ANALYSIS

Data analysis can turn raw data into meaningful information. Data analysis is the process of studying, cleaning, and modeling data so that it can be used to discover information, draw conclusions, and help make decisions. In this activity, you will collect, organize, and model data so that it can be used for data analysis.

❯ **To begin, imagine that you work for a store that sells ice cream.** Your manager wants to know which flavors customers are most likely to buy and how much of each flavor he should order in the next shipment. How can you use data analysis to discover this information?

❯ **To start, you'll have to gather data. You can do this with a survey.** Ask 25 family members, friends, or classmates to name their favorite ice cream flavor. Record the data.

❯ **Next, to make sense of the data, it needs to be organized.** Select the type of chart you would like to use to organize the data—a line plot or a tally chart.

❯ **Once the data is organized on the line plot or tally chart, create a bar graph to visually present it.** Include a title and data labels for the graph.

❯ **Use the graph to answer the following questions.**

* What was the order of ice cream flavors from favorite to least favorite?
* What was the favorite ice cream flavor?
* Which two flavors should the store manager order the most?

Consider This!

A survey is one way to gather data for analysis. What other way could you gather data about which ice cream flavors the store's customers are most likely to buy?

Chapter 6

THE FUTURE OF BIG DATA

Not that long ago, few people could imagine how big data would change our lives. And in the future, data will continue to evolve, along with the ways we generate and use it. What technologies will develop to generate data? What new ways will emerge to use data? As data becomes more entwined in daily lives, our world will never be the same!

Most people agree that data is not going away any time soon. If you think we generate a lot of data now, wait to see how much there is in a few more years! As the number of handheld devices such as smartphones, tablets, and smartwatches increases, the amount of data that all of these devices create will also increase.

And that's just the beginning. As technology races forward, more and more devices will be collecting, sharing, and using data from the world around us.

ESSENTIAL QUESTION

How do the benefits and risks of big data weigh against each other?

INTERNET OF THINGS

Have you ever heard of the **Internet of Things (IoT)**? Technology experts predict that the IoT is going to be a huge generator of data in the not-so-distant future.

WORDS TO KNOW

Internet of Things (IoT): everyday devices that are connected to the internet and have tiny sensors that gather, store, and process data.

thermostat: a device that automatically regulates temperature.

What exactly is the IoT? Well, have you heard of a smart lock, smart **thermostat**, or smart light? All these everyday objects are part of the IoT. They are connected to the internet and each other. They are embedded with tiny sensors that gather, store, and process data. Software manages each device's operation and makes decisions on how to respond to data.

Because they are linked to the internet, these devices can upload their data for more processing and analysis.

Devices that are part of the IoT aren't the normal computers and laptops that you use to surf the web. The IoT generally consists of devices that have traditionally not been connected to the internet or that can communicate with the internet without human action. That's why a smartphone is not considered an IoT device, but a fitness band can be part of the IoT.

An IoT device can be as simple as a child's toy or as complicated as a jet engine filled with thousands of sensors that collect and transmit data. Thanks to the IoT, billions of physical devices worldwide are connected to the internet, collecting and sharing data. Some experts predict that there will be more than 20 billion IoT devices in use by 2020.

How do you control the temperature at your house? Most people have a thermostat on the wall to set the indoor temperature. The thermostat sends a message to the furnace and air conditioning system to turn on or off based on the temperature it senses in the room. People can change the programmed temperature whenever they want, making it a little bit warmer or cooler based on their preferences.

DID YOU KNOW?

The Nest Learning Thermostat is one example of how the IoT can generate and use data.

The Nest Learning Thermostat changes this process. This system collects data about your day-to-day routines and the temperatures you like for certain days and times of the week. Then, it builds a schedule to program the home's heating and cooling accordingly—without you having to do anything.

Nest uses Wi-Fi to connect to the internet and your family's account. You can even monitor and adjust the Nest thermostat remotely from the website or through an app on your smartphone.

The smart thermostat works because it gathers a lot of data.

Unlike a traditional thermostat that uses a single sensor to measure the room's temperature, the Nest uses three temperature sensors to get a more accurate reading. A humidity sensor measures the moisture in the air. Motion and light sensors detect activity in the room. A Wi-Fi internet connection gathers weather data from the area.

Using all this data, Nest creates a schedule for the home's heating and cooling systems.

Learning to Play Checkers

Arthur Samuel (1901–1990) was one of the pioneers of machine learning. In the 1950s, he wrote a checkers-playing computer program. Using his program, Samuel had the computer play thousands of checkers games against itself. Over and over, the computer collected data about what types of board positions led to wins and which led to losses. The checkers-playing program learned what were good vs. bad board positions. With so much experience, the computer eventually learned enough to play checkers better than Samuel himself!

WORDS TO KNOW

glean: to collect.

spam filter: a program that decides which emails are important and which emails are junk.

emoji: a small digital image or icon used to express an idea or emotion.

hashtag: A word or phrase preceded by a hash sign (#) used on social media to identify messages on a specific topic.

MACHINE LEARNING

Experts predict that big data will drive advances in machine learning. Machine learning is a field of computer science that allows machines to learn and improve with experience, without being programmed by people.

Usually, you get a computer to perform a task by giving it a detailed set of instructions. That's what a computer program is—detailed instructions for a computer to follow. Machine learning does not use detailed instructions.

Instead, a computer learns how to perform a task by being given a set of examples of a task being done and learning from these examples.

To better understand this idea, think about how you could teach your younger brother to kick a ball. You might give him a set of detailed instructions. You'd tell him how far to lift his foot and what angle to place his ankle. You'd instruct him how far to bend his knee and how fast to move his leg. You'd tell him the exact order in which to do each step.

With a machine learning approach, instead of giving him instructions, you'd show your brother many examples of kicking a ball. You'd show him examples of different people kicking a ball and examples of people kicking different types of balls. Instead of telling him what to do, you'd teach him by showing him examples of people who know how to kick a ball. Which do you think would be more effective?

DID YOU KNOW?

Facebook's faces recognition feature, which automatically tags the friends it finds in your photos, is an example of machine learning in use.

Machine learning uses algorithms to **glean** information from data. The computer learns by looking for patterns in data that allow it to make better decisions in the future.

The goal of machine learning is for the computer to learn automatically, without a human explaining every step.

Through learning, the computer adjusts its actions appropriately. As the amount of data increases, the machine-learning algorithms improve their performance and predictions. Today, we are already using machine learning in many applications. Machine learning helps ride-sharing apps such as Uber and Lyft price rides and minimize wait times. Machine learning helps **spam filters** learn which emails to filter out of a person's inbox.

Even the social media site Instagram uses machine learning to identify the meaning of an **emoji**. With this information, Instagram can create and automatically suggest emojis and **hashtags** for users.

Detecting Water Waste

In Long Beach, California, water is a precious resource. In order to conserve water, local laws restrict the days and times residents and businesses can water their lawns. In the past, it was difficult for the city's water department to catch water wasters in the act. Traditional water meters measured how much water a customer used, but provided no information about how much water was used each day or what time of day a person used the most water. With smart water meters, the city and homeowners can get real-time data about water usage. These smart meters report water usage wirelessly over the web every five minutes. Having this data enables the city to detect illegal water usage as it happens. The data also helps homeowners conserve water. For example, one homeowner was able to cut her water bill by 88 percent after the smart meter data helped her discover a water leak under her home's foundation.

WORDS TO KNOW

chronic: recurring.

blood pressure: the pressure of the blood against the inner walls of the blood vessels.

biomedicine: medicine based on the application of the principles of the natural sciences and especially biology and biochemistry.

RFID: stands for radio frequency identification, a technology that uses electronic tags placed on objects to relay identifying information to an electronic reader using radio waves.

NEW USES FOR DATA

Already, many businesses are jumping on the data bandwagon. They are coming up with new ways to use data to understand and attract customers. Data is helping organizations make changes in their operations to be more efficient.

Data is not just for companies and governments. We use data from fitness trackers to track calorie consumption, activity levels, and sleep patterns. This information can help us make better health decisions.

In the future, there will be even more uses for data. In healthcare, smart watches and wearable devices could be used to collect data on millions of people and their various health conditions.

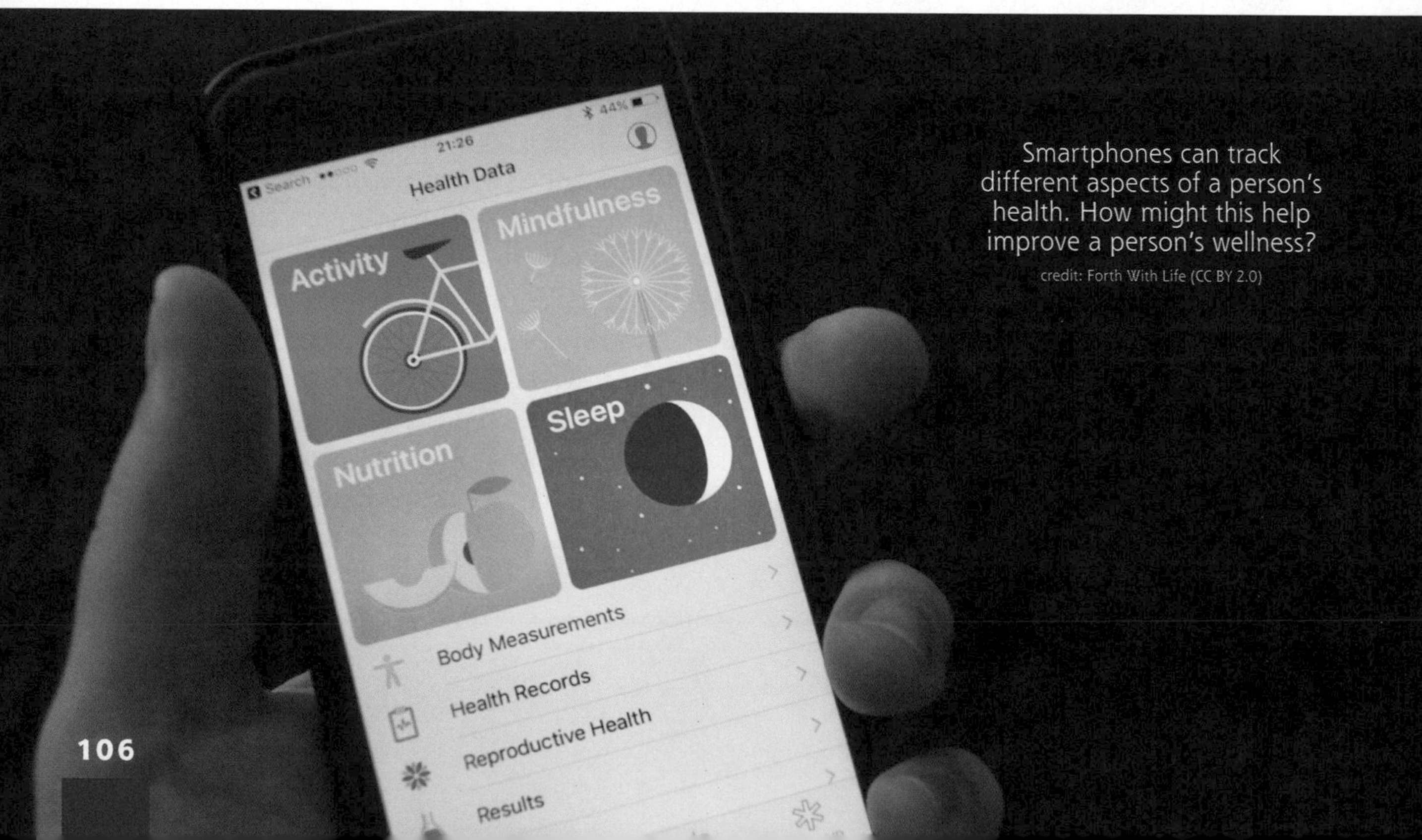

Smartphones can track different aspects of a person's health. How might this help improve a person's wellness?
credit: Forth With Life (CC BY 2.0)

Elderly people with **chronic** illnesses could be spared endless visits to a doctor's office—for example, a device could monitor their **blood pressure** and more and send this information automatically to the doctor. And with this massive pool of data, researchers may be better able to understand and predict disease and find new treatments.

For example, Apple's new health app, called ResearchKit, turns a smartphone into a **biomedical** research device. Researchers can collect data from users' phones to use for health studies. The phones might track how many steps a person takes each day or ask them to answer questions about how they feel after treatment or how a particular disease is progressing.

By making participation so easy, researchers might be able to significantly increase the number of people participating in studies, improving the accuracy of their results.

In Los Angeles, California, big data is helping police officers keep the community safe. In the Los Angeles Police Department's Real-Time Analysis and Critical Response Division, crime analysts and technology experts monitor lots of video screens. Some screens play news broadcasts, while others show real-time footage from around the city.

Hit the Slopes

The next time you go skiing, your lift ticket might be tracking your every move on the slopes. At some ski resorts, **RFID** tags inserted into lift tickets track skiers. The data helps the resorts understand wait times at the lifts, traffic patterns, and which lifts and runs are the most popular at what times of day. The tags can even track skiers if they become lost on the mountain. Resorts are also using data to send text alerts to customers to let them know when there is fresh powder snow on their favorite run or where the lift lines are the shortest.

You can see an interactive map of crime in Tucson, Arizona, at this website. Why might this be useful for citizens?

AZ Starnet crime

WORDS TO KNOW

seismic: relating to earthquakes.

predictive policing: the use of data to predict where and when certain types of crimes are going to occur.

neonatal: relating to newborn children.

Another screen tracks **seismic** activity in the area. At the center, a satellite map displays the locations of recent arrests in the city. Tracking crime data from a variety of sources, the police department uses an algorithm to predict where the next crime is most likely to occur.

The algorithm analyzes data to identify areas with high probabilities of certain crimes. Then, it places markers on city maps that are streamed to officers in patrol cars. This use of data, called **predictive policing**, is just one way that data is being used to prevent crime.

FUTURE CONCERNS

In recent years, the amount of data available from the internet, social media, smart phones, and many other sources has exploded. And it is expected to continuing growing at an incredible rate. Data has the potential to lead to important advances in many fields, from science and technology to health care and finance. Yet, at the same time, there are concerns that data could be misused.

credit: DonkeyHotey (CC BY 2.0)

One of the biggest concerns is privacy. Who owns all of the data that your fitness tracker, smart refrigerator, or smart car collect?

What would happen if the fitness tracker manufacturer sold data about your activity levels to your health insurer? The insurer might use this information to put you in a riskier insurance group and charge you more money.

In the same way, the car manufacturer might sell data from your smart car to your insurance carrier. The insurer might raise your rates or even drop you if they decide your driving habits are too risky. At what point is this a violation of your privacy?

In the future, society will have to make tough decisions on the ethical ways to use and not to use collected data.

In some cases, you might not even know that your data is being misused. Internet-connected smart toys can be manipulated by hackers. Security experts caution parents and children that computer-savvy strangers can hack into smart toys to gather personal data–such as a person's address, name, and birth date. They can download a child's photo. They can even listen to conversations in your home and record your voice.

Monitoring Sick Babies

Big data is already helping hospitals monitor sick and premature babies. At the Hospital for Sick Children in Toronto, Canada, babies in the **neonatal** intensive care unit are at high risk for infection. Researchers from the University of Ontario found a way to record and analyze millions of sick babies' heartbeats and breathing patterns. They developed an algorithm that can predict infections 24 hours before physical symptoms emerge. With this information, doctors and nurses can monitor their littlest patients. When the algorithm predicts infection, the medical team can start treating the babies earlier, improving their chances of survival.

WORDS TO KNOW

bias: a way of looking at or thinking about something that might be wrong or unfair or limiting.

Another concern is people using big data for their personal benefit. When people know that a set of data is being used to make an important decision, they have a motive to try to manipulate it to get the best result for them personally. For example, college administrators have made decisions that not everyone agrees with in order to improve their school's national rankings, such as investing in state-of-the-art gyms at the expense of classrooms and academics. Do you think this is a good idea?

What happens if data is not accurate? When data is **biased** or inaccurate, it can lead to bad decisions or wrong conclusions.

For example, in the 2016 U.S. presidential election, most polling groups predicted for months that the Democratic candidate Hillary Clinton would win.

After Donald Trump won the election, many people asked why the data was wrong. Some news outlets reported that pollsters struggled to find people to provide data for their polls because they called only landline phones, even though many Americans use cell phones instead. This is one factor that may have led to a biased data set on which pollsters based their election predictions.

DID YOU KNOW?

In 2017, Coca Cola announced the launch of Cherry Sprite, a new soda flavor based on monitoring data from self-service soft drink machines that allow customers to mix their own soda.

Big data has the potential to change the way we live, work, and think. Harnessing this data can lead to many exciting technologies and advances. It can help us do what we already do better. And it will help us do new and amazing things. At the same time, we need to understand the risks that a data-driven world faces so that we can use data in the best ways possible.

ESSENTIAL QUESTION

How do the benefits and risks of big data weigh against each other?

Activity

INTERNET OF THINGS—A POSITIVE OR NEGATIVE TECHNOLOGY?

The IoT connects everyday devices such as refrigerators, stoves, and cars to the internet and uses software to link them to our daily lives. To do their jobs, IoT devices rely on data that they collect all day, every day.

The IoT can make daily life a lot easier. But there's a downside to all this connectivity. What if someone in your neighborhood is able to hack into your freezer and turn it off as a prank? All of your ice cream melts! What are some other ways the IoT can backfire?

- **Think about the positive effects of the IoT.** How can connected devices and the data they generate improve our lives and society as a whole?
- **Now consider the negative aspects of the IoT.** What risks arise from these devices and the data they generate?
- **Do you think the IoT will help or harm society in the future?** Why do you believe this? Come up with at least three points to support your position.
- **Write a brief essay that explains your point of view on the IoT.** Be sure to include an introductory paragraph, separate paragraphs for each of your three main points, and a conclusion. Share your essay with your class.

Try This!

Write a persuasive essay taking the other side. Use your essay to convince the reader to agree with your position.

Activity

MACHINES VS. HUMANS

Data can be used to help people make better decisions. Should all decisions be ruled by data and machines? Or are some decisions still better off being made by a human being?

Read some background information about artificial intelligence and human decision-making. As you research the issue, think about the following questions.

* What types of decision-making are machines good at? What qualities do machines have that make them better decision-makers than humans? What drawbacks are there to machine-based decisions?

* What types of decision-making are humans good at? What qualities do humans have that make them better decision-makers than machines? What drawbacks are there to human-based decisions?

* What role, if any, should intuition, experience, emotion, judgment, and **morality** have in decision-making?

DID YOU KNOW?

In a 2016 survey of 2,100 business decision-makers by a company called PwC, 41 percent said they rely more on computers and algorithms than their own experience, **intuition**, and judgment.

Prepare for a debate on the following question: Are machines better than humans at making decisions?

As you prepare, note the points you will make to support your argument. Then, try to think of what the opposing side might say against you and prepare responses.

Try This!

Prepare a PowerPoint presentation taking the other side of the debate. Use your presentation to persuade the reader to agree with your position.

WORDS TO KNOW

intuition: the ability to understand something right away.

morality: the distinction between right and wrong and good and bad.

Activity

HOW WILL WE USE DATA IN THE FUTURE?

Throughout the years, advances in technology have allowed people to track more data than at any other time in the past. Technology advances have also created new ways to analyze and use data. As technology continues to advance, people will discover new ways to collect, analyze, and use data.

› **Think about new types of data that people will be able to collect in the future.** Choose an industry to research—health care, banking, manufacturing, retail, insurance, media and entertainment, sports, education, or government. How does this industry currently collect and use data?

› **Think about ways that the types of data collected by this industry might change in the future.** Where will it come from? How will it be collected? What role will technology have in data collection and analysis? In what new ways will the industry use the data? Come up with at least three future changes in data collection or use.

› **Write a short essay that explains your research on how the use of data will change in the industry in the future.** Be sure to include an introductory paragraph, separate paragraphs for each of your three main points, and a conclusion. Share your essay with your class.

Try This!

Choose another industry to research and repeat the activity. How are the two industries different from each other? How do their differences reflect the ways each industry uses data?

abundance: a very large quantity of something.

accuracy: free from mistake or error.

actuary: a person who compiles and analyzes statistics and uses them to calculate insurance risks and premiums.

algorithm: a set of steps or a procedure to be followed in calculations or other problem-solving operations, especially by a computer.

Analytical Engine: a proposed mechanical general-purpose computer designed by English mathematician Charles Babbage.

analyze: to study and examine.

artificial intelligence (AI): the intelligence of a computer, program, or machine.

BCE: put after a date, BCE stands for Before Common Era and counts down to zero. CE stands for Common Era and counts up from zero. These nonreligious terms correspond to BC and AD. This book was printed in 2018 CE.

bias: a way of looking at or thinking about something that might be wrong or unfair or limiting.

big data: data sets that are enormous and complex.

binary: a math system that uses only the numbers 0 and 1.

biomedicine: medicine based on the application of the principles of the natural sciences and especially biology and biochemistry.

blood pressure: the pressure of the blood against the inner walls of the blood vessels.

byte: a group of eight bits that is treated as a single piece of information.

capacitor: a device that stores electrical energy until it's needed.

carbon copy: an exact copy of a document made using carbon paper between two or more pieces of paper.

census: the process of acquiring and recording information about the members of a given population.

central processing unit (CPU): the part of a computer in which operations are controlled and executed.

chronic: recurring.

circuit: a path for electric current to flow, beginning and ending at the same point.

commission: an instruction given to another person, such as an artist, for a piece of work.

concentric: having a common center.

coordinate: to bring different parts of a system or process together.

correlation: a connection between two things.

cuneiform: a system of wedge-shaped letters created by ancient civilizations.

data analytics: the process of examining data to draw conclusions about it.

database: a collection of data that can be easily searched.

database management system (DBMS): a software program that handles the storage, retrieval, and updating of data in a computer system.

data: facts and observations about something.

data mining: the use of models to automatically search through large amounts of data.

data point: a discrete unit of information.

decimal: a number system based on units of 10.

diagnose: to determine the identity and cause of a disease or problem.

Difference Engine: an early calculating machine, designed and partially built during the early 1800s by English mathematician Charles Babbage.

digital: involving the use of computer technology and presenting data as numbers.

durable: able to last.

emoji: a small digital image or icon used to express an idea or emotion.

engineer: a person who uses math, science, and creativity to solve problems or meet human needs.

estimate: to form a general idea about the value, size, or cost of something.

ethical: doing the right thing.

evolve: to change or develop gradually.

flash drive: a small, portable device that stores data.

flash technology: data storage technology that uses electrical energy to store data.

fraud: the crime of using dishonest methods to take something valuable away from someone else.

glean: to collect.

global positioning system (GPS): a system of satellites, computers, and receivers that can determine the exact location of a receiver anywhere on the planet.

hacker: an expert at programming and solving problems on a computer. Also describes someone who illegally gains access to and sometimes tampers with information in a computer system.

hashtag: A word or phrase preceded by a hash sign (#) used on social media to identify messages on a specific topic.

humidity: the amount of moisture in the air.

Industrial Revolution: a period of time beginning in the late 1700s when people started using machines to make things in large factories.

influence: to affect the character, development, or outcome of something.

influenza: a highly infectious disease that causes fever, sore throat, muscle aches, and fatigue.

infographic: a visual representation of data, information, or knowledge.

innovative: introducing new ideas and creative thinking.

insurance: a contract in which an individual or entity receives financial protection or reimbursement against losses from an insurance company.

integrated circuit: a tiny complex of electronic components and their connections on a small piece of material such as silicon.

interactive: having a two-way flow of information between a computer and a user.

Internet of Things (IoT): everyday devices that are connected to the internet and have tiny sensors that gather, store, and process data.

intuition: the ability to understand something right away.

keyword: a word or phrase that describes online content.

machine learning: a field of computer science that teaches a computer to perform a task by giving it a set of examples.

magnetism: the force that attracts or repels between magnets.

malicious: intending to do harm.

median: the middle value in a list of numbers.

memory card: a type of storage device that is used for storing media and data files.

Mesopotamia: an ancient civilization located between the Tigris and Euphrates Rivers, in what today is part of Iraq.

microprocessor: a small electronic chip that manages information and controls what a computer does.

mode: the number that appears most often in a set of numbers.

monitor: to watch or keep track of something or someone.

morality: the distinction between right and wrong and good and bad.

neonatal: relating to newborn children.

nonprofit: an organization supported by donations whose main mission is to help people, animals, the environment, or other causes.

optical storage: a type of data storage that uses lasers to record and retrieve data.

outlier: a person or thing apart or detached from the main body or system.

pandemic: a worldwide spread of disease.

parallel processing: using more than one processor in the same computer.

pictograph: the symbols in the first written languages, based on pictures instead of letters.

pixel: short for "picture element," one of the small squares of color used to show an image on a digital screen.

platter: a large, circular plate in a magnetic hard drive that stores data via magnetic charges.

predictive modeling: a process that uses data mining and probability to forecast outcomes.

predictive policing: the use of data to predict where and when certain types of crimes are going to occur.

processed data: facts that have been edited or cleaned in some way after collection.

programmer: a person who writes computer programs. Also called a coder.

protocols: a set of rules governing the exchange or transmission of data between devices.

prototype: a model of something that allows engineers to test their idea.

punch card: a card with holes punched in it that gives directions to a machine or computer.

qualitative data: facts about something's qualities.

quantitative data: facts that can be measured and reported in numbers.

random access memory (RAM): a very fast temporary data storage system that computers use to hold the data they are manipulating.

range: the difference between the highest and lowest values in a set of numbers.

raw data: facts that have not been analyzed in any way.

read-write head: a small part of the disk drive that transforms a magnetic field into electrical current or vice versa.

relational database: a database structured to recognize relationships among separately stored pieces of data.

relay: an electrical device that is activated by a current or signal in one circuit to open or close another circuit.

remote server: a computer that provides data to other computers and is located in a different physical location.

RFID: stands for radio frequency identification, a technology that uses electronic tags placed on objects to relay identifying information to an electronic reader using radio waves.

rubric: a guide listing specific criteria for grading or scoring academic papers, projects, or tests.

scribe: a person who copies books, letters, and other documents by hand.

search engine: a program that searches for the keywords identified by the user.

search query: a question or query that a person enters into an internet search engine.

sectors: smaller segments of tracks on a magnetic hard drive.

segment: part of something.

seismic: relating to earthquakes.

semiconducting: a material that can only weakly conduct electricity.

simultaneously: at the same time.

social service program: a program designed to promote social welfare, such as feeding and housing people living in poverty.

solar power: energy from the sun converted to electricity.

spam filter: a program that decides which emails are important and which emails are junk.

statistics: the practice or science of collecting and analyzing numerical data in large quantities.

stereotype: the inaccurate belief that all people who share a single physical or cultural trait are the same.

structured data: data that is organized in a pre-determined way, such as a field in a database record.

Sumerian: a group of people living in ancient Mesopotamia, which is modern-day Iraq.

symbolic assembly language: a programming language that lets users relay information to computers with words instead of numbers.

tabulate: to count, record, or list data in a systematic way.

tally: to count the number of something.

targeted: directed at a group.

technology: the scientific or mechanical tools, methods, and systems used to solve a problem or do work.

tenant: someone who pays rent to use land or buildings owned by someone else.

thermostat: a device that automatically regulates temperature.

tracks: circular paths on the platter of a magnetic hard drive.

trajectory: the curve or line taken by an object moving through space.

transistor: a small device that acts as an on/off switch to control the flow of electricity in a computer.

unprecedented: never done or known before.

unstructured data: data that is not organized in a predetermined way, such as a photograph.

urban: relating to a city or large town.

vaccine: medicine designed to keep a person from getting a particular disease, usually given by needle.

vacuum tube: an electronic component that looks like a lightbulb and was used as an on/off switch in early computers and other appliances.

variety: the number of different data sources and types of data.

velocity: the rate at which data is generated and changed.

virus: a program that enters your computer and damages or destroys stored information. Also a non-living microbe that can cause disease.

visualization: to put something in a picture or other visual format.

volume: the quantity of data available today.

wearable: an electronic device that can be worn on the body, either as an accessory or as part of material used in clothing.

web analytics: software programs that track, collect, analyze, and report data about website traffic.

Metric Conversions

Use this chart to find the metric equivalents to the English measurements in this book. If you need to know a half measurement, divide by two. If you need to know twice the measurement, multiply by two. How do you find a quarter measurement? How do you find three times the measurement?

English	Metric
1 inch	2.5 centimeters
1 foot	30.5 centimeters
1 yard	0.9 meter
1 mile	1.6 kilometers
1 pound	0.5 kilogram
1 teaspoon	5 milliliters
1 tablespoon	15 milliliters
1 cup	237 milliliters

BOOKS

Beevor, Lucy. *The Invention of the Computer* (World-Changing Inventions). Capstone, 2018.

Eboch, M.M. *Big Data and Privacy Rights* (Essential Library of the Information Age). ABDO, 2016.

Erwig, Martin. *Once Upon an Algorithm: How Stories Explain Computing*. MIT Press, 2017.

Freedman, Jeri. *When Companies Spy on You: Corporate Data Mining and Big Business* (Spying, Surveillance, and Privacy in the 21st Century). Cavendish Square, 2017.

Hand, Carol. *How the Internet Changed History* (Essential Library of Inventions). ABDO, 2015.

Mozer, Mindy. *Big Data and You* (Digital and Information Literacy). Rosen, 2014.

Steffens, Bradley. *Big Data Analyst* (Cutting Edge Careers). ReferencePoint Press, 2017.

MUSEUMS

Twentieth-Century Technology Museum: *20thcenturytech.com*

American Computer and Robotics Museum: *compustory.com*

Charles Babbage Institute: *cbi.umn.edu*

Computer History Museum: *computerhistory.org*

InfoAge Science History Learning Center: *infoage.org*

Living Computer Museum: *livingcomputers.org*

MIT Museum: *mitmuseum.mit.edu*

Smithsonian's Museum of American History, Computers and Mathematics Collections: *americanhistory.si.edu*

WEBSITES

CompTIA Association of IT Professionals (AITP): *aitp.org*

Data.gov: *data.gov*

Data Science 101: *101.datascience.community*

Data Science Central: *datasciencecentral.com*

IEEE Computer Society: *computer.org*

National Park Service: Computing Kids & Data Science: *nps.gov/kids/features/2015/edweek.cfm*

QR CODE GLOSSARY

page 3: *domo.com/learn/* data-never-sleeps-5?aid=DPR072517

page 16: *nces.ed.gov/nceskids/createagraph*

page 20: *nationalarchives.gov.uk/domesday*

page 35: *computerhistory.org*

page 36: *computerhistory.org/revolution/punched-cards/2/2/2395*

page 36: *computerhistory.org/revolution/memory-storage/8/326/32*

page 39: *physics.smu.edu/fattarus/zuse_z1.html*

page 49: *youtube.com/watch?v=WABAIJHPdnw*

page 58: *convertbinary.com/alphabet*

page 62: *intel.com/content/dam/www/public/us/en/documents/case-studies/* big-data-xeon-e5-trustway-case-study.pdf

page 64: *techrepublic.com/article/* farming-for-the-future-how-one-company-uses-big-data-to-maximize-yields-and-minimize-impact

page 71: *google.org/flutrends/about*

page 75: *asc.upenn.edu/sites/default/files/TradeoffFallacy_1.pdf*

page 76: *archive.org*

page 76: *earth.nullschool.net*

page 76: *csc.ncsu.edu/faculty/healey/tweet_viz/tweet_app*

page 76: *afdc.energy.gov/locator/stations*

page 96: *duelingdata.blogspot.co.uk/* 2016/01/the-beatles.html

page 96: *thedailyviz.com/2016/09/17/how-common-is-your-birthday-dailyviz*

page 96: *kidsdiscover.com/infographics/infographic-volcanoes-inside*

page 96: *thelogocompany.net/blog/infographics/psychology-color-logo-design*

page 97: *venngage.com/blog/* 9-types-of-infographic-template/

page 107: *dynamic.azstarnet.com/crime*

ESSENTIAL QUESTIONS

Introduction: In what ways does data affect your everyday life?

Chapter 1: What areas in your life involve data?

Chapter 2: What might the world be like if we were still using pen and paper to record all our data?

Chapter 3: What would it be like to try and use data without a data management system to help you?

Chapter 4: How can big data put us at risk? How can it help?

Chapter 5: Why is data easier to understand when it's in a visual format?

Chapter 6: How do the benefits and risks of big data weigh against each other?

A

activities
- Changing How We Live, 33
- Chart Your Thanksgiving Traditions, 90–91
- Collect Data for Analysis, 92–93
- Design a Poll, 7
- Explore Weather Data, 16–17
- Exploring Data Analysis, 99
- Finding Big Data, 76–77
- How Will We Use Data in the Future?, 113
- Info Through Infographics, 96–97
- Internet of Things - A Positive or Negative Technology?, 111
- Interpreting Big Data, 79
- Learning about Computer History, 35
- Machines vs. Humans, 112
- Make a Paper Database, 56–57
- Privacy vs. Convenience, 75
- Quantitative vs. Qualitative Data in School, 15
- Representing Data with Graphs, 94–95
- Send a Message in Binary Code, 58
- Storing Color as Data, 54–55
- Tell a Story in Pictographs, 34
- Using Big Data to Target Customers, 78
- Using Punch Cards to Store Data, 36–37
- What's the Most Popular Skittle?, 98
- Where's the Data, 6
- Working with Binary Numbers, 52–53

adding machines, iv, 23–24
Advanced Research Projects Agency (ARPA), v, 31
Amazon, 46
Analytical Engine, iv, 25
Apple, v, 30, 46, 107
Atanasof-Berry Computer (ABC), 25–26
Atanasoff, John Vincent, 25

B

Babbage, Charles, iv, 24–25
Berners-Lee, Timothy John, v, 32
Berry, Clifford, 25
big data
- analysis of. *See* data analytics
- dangers or disadvantages of, 71–75, 108–110
- definition and description of, 2, 59
- future of, 100–113
- health care and, v, 8, 12–13, 14, 63, 64, 68–71, 106–107, 109. *See also* fitness data
- power and importance of, 63
- privacy and security issues with, 72–75, 108–109
- social media and, v, 61, 66–67, 88, 104, 105
- sources of, 61, 76–77
- storage of. *See* data storage
- understanding, 80–99
- users of, 64–66, 83–85
- uses of, 11–14, 62–63, 76–77, 106–108, 113
- volume, velocity, and variety of, 60

Bilas, Fran, 26
binary numbers/code, 29, 30, 39–40, 48, 52–55, 57–58
Burroughs, William S., iv, 24

C

census data, iv, 2, 11, 19–22
Chico's, 84
cloud storage, v, 47
color, 9, 39, 54–55, 81, 98
compact discs, v, 49
computers
- binary numbers/code for, 29, 30, 39–40, 48, 52–55, 57–58
- data analysis using, 82, 85–87, 93. *See also* data analytics
- data storage in, iv–v, 4, 11, 38–58. *See also* big data; digital data
- flash drives/storage for, v, 41, 42, 44–45
- hard drives of, 41, 42–43, 50
- history and evolution of, iv–v, 24–33, 35
- internet and, v, 31–32, 47, 88
- machine learning by, 87, 103, 104–105
- quantum, 30
- random access memory of, 46

counting methods, iv, 20, 21–22, 23–24, 40. *See also* computers
crime data, 107–108
cuneiform, 18

D

data
analysis of. *See* data analytics
definition and description of, 1, 8
digital. *See* big data; digital data
history and evolution of, iv–v, 18–37
power and importance of, 3–4, 63
qualitative, 2, 9, 15
quantitative, 2, 9, 15
raw vs. processed, 13, 63, 65, 76, 82. *See also* data analytics
sources of, 2–3, 8–17, 61, 76–77
storage of. *See* data storage
structured vs. unstructured, 73
uses of, 11–14, 62–63, 76–77, 106–108, 113
data analytics
data interpretation and, 79
definition of, 65, 82
process of, 85–87
of social media data, 67
of sports data, 66, 77
of statistics, 8
understanding big data via, 82–87, 88–89, 92–93, 99
users of data benefiting from, 64–66, 83–85
uses of data based on, 11, 13, 14, 62–63
web analytics as, 88–89
databases, 50–51, 56–57, 73, 85
data mining, 87–88
data storage
compact discs for, v, 49
digital, iv–v, 4, 11, 38–58
flash drives/storage for, v, 41, 42, 44–45
hard drives for, 41, 42–43, 50
management and organization of, 49–51, 53, 56–57
online or cloud storage for, v, 47
optical storage for, v, 45
paper or non-digital, iv, 11, 18–25, 34, 36–37
quantities of data and, 4
units or bytes of, 48
Difference Engine, 24
digital data
big data as. *See* big data.
quantity of, 3–4, 10–11, 60
storage of, iv–v, 4, 11, 38–58
uses of, 12–13, 62–63, 76–77, 106–108, 113
Domesday Book, iv, 20

E

Eckert, J. Presper, iv, 26, 27
educational data, 8, 64
Eisenhower, Dwight D., 27, 31
Electronic Discrete Variable Automatic Computer (EDVAC), 27, 28
Electronic Numerical Integrator and Calculator (ENIAC), iv, 26–27, 28
engineering design process, 5
environmental data, 64
essential questions, 5, 14, 32, 51, 74, 89, 110

F

Facebook, v, 46, 66, 104
Felt, Dorr E., iv, 24
fitness data, 3, 10, 14, 61, 102, 108–109
flash drives/storage, v, 41, 42, 44–45
future of big data, 100–113

G

global positioning system (GPS) data, 12, 66
Google, v, 30, 32, 46, 70–71
Google Analytics, 93
graphs and charts, 16, 65, 81, 86, 87, 90–91, 94–95, 99
Gutenberg, Johannes, 23

H

Hadoop, 93
hard drives, 41, 42–43, 50
health care data, v, 8, 12–13, 14, 63, 64, 68–71, 106–107, 109. *See also* fitness data
history of data, iv–v, 18–37
Hollerith, Herman, iv, 21–22
Hopper, Grace Murray, iv, 27

I

IBM, iv–v, 30
infographics, 3, 81, 87, 96–97
Intel, 29–30
internet, v, 31–32, 47, 88
Internet of Things (IoT), 101–103, 105, 111

J

Jacquard, Joseph Marie, 37
Jenning, Betty, 26

K

Knight, Nancy, 17

L

Leibniz, Gottfried Wilhelm, 40
Lenovo, 84–85
location and routing data, 12, 65–66, 83, 107
Lovelace, Ada (Byron), iv, 25

M

machine learning, 87, 103, 104–105
Macy's, 67
maps, 12, 66, 81, 83, 107
Mauchly, John, iv, 26
McNulty, Kay, 26

N

Nest Learning Thermostat, 103
NoSQL, 93

O

online data storage, v, 47
optical storage, v, 45

P

parallel processing, 29
Phi Yü Ching, 19
pictographs, 18, 34, 91
polls, 7, 110. *See also* surveys
predictive data, iv, 17, 27, 63, 64, 69–71, 77, 86, 87–88, 89, 108, 109–110
printing press, 23
privacy issues, 72–75, 108–109
processed data, 13, 63. *See also* data analytics
punch cards, iv, 21–22, 25, 36–37

Q

qualitative data, 2, 9, 15
quantitative data, 2, 9, 15
quantum computers, 30

R

random access memory (RAM), 46
raw data, 13, 63, 65, 76, 82
retail data, 4, 61, 64, 65, 67, 72, 73, 75, 78, 82–85

S

Samuel, Arthur, 103
security of data, 74, 109
Sloan Digital Sky Survey, 10, 11
Snyder, Betty, 26
social media data, v, 61, 66–67, 88, 104, 105
sports data, 8, 64, 66, 77, 107
structured data, 73
surveys, 7, 10, 11, 99. *See also* polls
swine flu (H1N1) data, v, 68–71

T

tax data, 1, 2, 18, 20, 22
Thomas de Colmar, Charles Xavier, iv, 23
timeline, iv–v
transportation data, 62. *See also* location and routing data
typewriters, iv, 22–23

U

understanding big data
- data analytics for, 82–87, 88–89, 92–93, 99
- data mining for, 87–88
- importance of, 80
- visualization for, 81, 86–87, 90–91, 94–97
- web analytics for, 88–89

United Parcel Service (UPS), 65–66
UNIVAC (UNIVersal Automatic Computer), iv, 27
unstructured data, 73

V

visualization of data, 81, 86–87, 90–91, 94–97. *See also* graphs and charts; infographics; maps; pictographs
von Neumann, John, 27

W

wearables, 14, 106–107
weather/climate data, 8, 16–17, 64–65, 86
web analytics, 88–89
Wescoff, Marlyn, 26

Z

Z1 computer, 39
Zuse, Konrad, 39